Everything Changes Everything

Also by Lauren Kessler:

Free: Two Years, Six Lives, and the Long Journey Home

A Grip of Time: When Prison Is Your Life

The Write Path: Essays on the Art of Writing and the Joy of Reading

Raising the Barre: Big Dreams, False Starts, and My Midlife Quest to Dance The Nutcracker

Counter Clockwise: My Year of Hypnosis, Hormones, Dark Chocolate, and Other Adventures in the World of Anti-Aging

My Teenage Werewolf: A Mother, a Daughter, a Journey Through the Thicket of Adolescence

Dancing with Rose: Finding Life in the Land of Alzheimer's

Clever Girl: Elizabeth Bentley, the Spy Who Ushered in the McCarthy Era

The Happy Bottom Riding Club: The Life and Times of Pancho Barnes

Full Court Press: A Season in the Life of a Winning Basketball Team and the Women Who Made It Happen

Stubborn Twig: Three Generations in the Life of a Japanese American Family

After All These Years: Sixties Ideals in a Different World

Everything Changes Everything

Love, Loss, and a Really Long Walk: A Memoir

Lauren Kessler

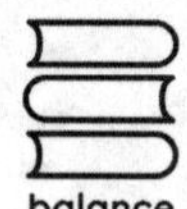

NEW YORK BOSTON

Balance
Hachette Book Group
1290 Avenue of the Americas
New York, NY 10104
GCP-Balance.com
@GCPBalance

First Edition: February 2026

Balance is an imprint of Grand Central Publishing. The Balance name and logo are registered trademarks of Hachette Book Group, Inc.

Print book interior design by Marie Mundaca.

Library of Congress Control Number: 2025025501

ISBNs: 978-0-306-83575-9 (hardcover), 978-0-306-83577-3 (ebook)

Printed in the United States of America

LSC-C

Printing 1, 2025

For Tom,
here,
there,
everywhere

and for Lizzie,
may you find your way home

No hay camino,
se hace camino al andar.
There is no road,
you make your own path as you walk.

—Antonio Machado

The idea is not to paper over your loss . . . the idea is smaller than that, yet also grander: that after all the grief and loss and disruption you are still—you always will be—exactly who you are.

—Susan Cain, *Bittersweet*

Author's Note

THIS IS A WORK of nonfiction—and it is also a memoir. Everything in it is fact-based, grounded in research, or drawn from direct experience. But every observation, every memory, every moment has passed through me. And that makes it subjective.

Memoir and nonfiction are often seen as opposites: one memory-inspired and personal, the other objective and reportorial. I reject that dichotomy.

All the people in this book are real. I have not invented or combined characters, nor knowingly altered any facts about their lives. I have used initials in place of names for the two men in Lizzie's life and for my back-in-the-day boyfriends.

The events in this book are real. Most I witnessed (and lived through) firsthand and documented in real time. Others I reconstructed using notes, emails, texts, photos, and documents. I have not altered details to "assist" the narrative.

The dialogue comes from direct observation (and participation), contemporaneous documentation, or memory assisted by my own journal entries, photographs, and interviews. I have rendered it as faithfully as I could. I invented nothing.

I've done my best to offer both facts and insight—the reportorial and the personal—with accuracy and care. I have actively struggled with the complexity of memory, emotion, and lived experience. It's life, after all.

Prologue

"BECAUSE I STILL MATTER," one older woman said.

"Because I need to figure out what matters," said a young man.

"Because I need time to think."

"Because I think too much."

There were maybe thirty of us sitting on wooden chairs, crowded together in the little interior courtyard of the Iglesia de Santa Maria in the medieval town of Carrión de los Condos. It was the late afternoon of my sixteenth day walking the Camino Francés. One of the four Augustinian nuns who would be leading us in song had asked us to say why we were on this journey, this iconic ancient pilgrimage walked by tens of thousands from around the world every year.

I wanted to say something simple, like the others before me

had said, but it wasn't simple. It didn't form into a single sentence. It was an answer entangled in backstory. And not just my backstory. All of ours. I had both clarity and confusion about why I had traveled almost six thousand miles to walk five hundred miles. How I could be both clear and confused was, well, confusing. But then it was my turn.

"I need to do something to separate the life I've been living from the life that is now in front of me," is what I ended up saying. And then I added, unnecessarily, given who we all were in that courtyard and what we had all experienced before we put down our backpacks to sit in this space: "And it needed to be something big."

As I was to learn, there are many moments on the Camino that grab hold of you, that surprise you, that sandblast you. This was one of those moments: Saying those words aloud, admitting the enormity of this transition, the blank canvas of the future. Being in the presence—and oh, man, was it a presence—of these nuns, one of whom was so beatific that it was easy to imagine she had been touched by God. Even if you didn't believe there was a God. Sitting in the fading sun with people from around the world, people you didn't know, but in that moment you knew intimately. Turning my head to see Kiki, our white-hot friendship still in its early days, both of us tearing up as we sang "Amazing Grace." And then, after songs sung by pilgrims—that's what we walkers are called—from Italy, France, Germany, Sweden, Australia, South Korea, and elsewhere, the nuns led us in the final song, in Spanish, the refrain of which went like this: *Todo cambia todo.* Everything changes everything.

And it does.

For some people, you say *the Camino*, and they get all excited. They know exactly what you're talking about. They've been wanting to walk the Camino for years. It's on their bucket list. Not me. I do not have a bucket list, nor had I ever heard of the Camino until I met Lydia, a documentarian who was working on a project featuring one of the men I had mentored when I ran a writers' group in a maximum security prison. She had produced and directed a film back in 2013 that traced the journeys of six people who walked the most popular of the many Camino pilgrimages, the Francés. It was, I learned, a five-hundred-mile trek across northern Spain beginning in a small town in France at the foothills of the Pyrenees and ending dramatically in front of the massive Romanesque/Gothic/baroque Archcathedral Basilica of Santiago de Compostela in the Galician city of Santiago de Compostela. This was where, it was said, the remains of Saint James, one of Christ's apostles, were enshrined. Since the early Middle Ages, Catholic pilgrims had walked this and other caminos. There are seven well-established routes of Saint James in Europe.

I knew nothing of this. I was not a Catholic. I was not looking for a spiritual awakening. Or maybe I was and I didn't know it. What I told myself was that I needed something hard to do that I *chose* to do instead of something hard to do that came out of nowhere and gobsmacked me. I had been gobsmacked. I was living in a country that had been gobsmacked, in a world that had been gobsmacked. What I told myself was that I needed a "time out of time," a solitary, immersive adventure, a physical, logistical, emotional challenge that would catapult me out of my life. But not just out of *my* life; out of what had become of our collective lives. Where I wanted to be catapulted to, I had no idea.

I didn't do much research, which was unusual for me. I am generally a glutton for research in both my professional and personal lives. I envision. I make lists. I plan. I curate. I schedule. I delight in the descent into the intricacies of detail. But this was different. It had to be different. Because everything was different. The challenge of doing this would not just be the physical challenge of walking five hundred miles. It would be the challenge of allowing the experience to wash over me, of ceding control. I had learned the hard way—hadn't we all?—that control was an illusion.

What I knew about the Camino I gleaned from Lydia's film, a few websites, and Wikipedia. I knew that the route scaled mountains and dipped into valleys, that it meandered across undulating plains, roamed through olive groves and vineyards, and ventured across both arid flatlands and green rolling hills. I read the descriptions. I knew there were churches, chapels, monasteries, convents, wayside shrines, and holy fountains along the way. But I didn't delve into the history. I knew that small villages, many of them ancient way stations and pilgrim outposts, dotted the landscape. I knew that I would occasionally come upon a town of some size: Pamplona, Burgos, León. But these were just names to me. I didn't view Google images. I didn't want to know what I would see. I didn't join an online pilgrims' group. I didn't even watch the apparently iconic movie that I was to discover was viewed (and endlessly referenced) by every single person I met along the way, Martin Sheen's *The Way*.

I did pay some attention to the necessities. I am, after all, a grown-up. I spent time figuring out how to get to the hard-to-get-to starting place of the Camino Francés, the small village of Saint-Jean-Pied-de-Port on the French side of the Pyrenees. I spent time figuring out (although not as successfully as I thought I had) what I needed to bring along on the trek. I would be carrying everything on my back. On the Camino, what one carries is not just, or most importantly, about the ultralight backpack and the bamboo walking poles, the nylon hiking pants and rain jacket chosen by weight, not fashion. I did do *that* research. But I hadn't spent much time delving into the other baggage I would carry, the emotional heft, the weight of all that had happened. I knew I was carrying more than I ever had before, but I chose not to probe too deeply. There was too much *there* there.

Although I thought about the daily "stages" of the walk—the guidebooks segmented the journey this way—I didn't plan how much I'd walk every day or where I'd stop that night. I did try to estimate how long the entire journey might take. I had to book a return flight. But in between arrival and departure, there existed a mostly blank canvas. This weight I was carrying, not the backpack weight, the other kind . . . I needed to allow myself to acknowledge it, to sift through it, feel it, figure out what could be left by the wayside, and then find my new center of gravity. Truthfully, I am not sure I thought big thoughts like this then. I think them now, two years after the journey's end. Back then, I just knew I wanted to go. I needed to go. I wanted to see what shape I was in after everything that had happened, and not just to me. To us.

Because it was not one thing. It was everything. It was Tom. It was Lizzie. It was this fraught post-9/11, postpandemic life we were all struggling to make sense of. It was that, for me, life had become unrecognizable. And I thought: *Maybe just putting one foot in front of another and trudging across vast landscapes and thinking only of where I am going to sleep that night, and meeting strangers who don't know about my husband and my daughter, maybe walking without a history, walking without a past, maybe that will help.*

Maybe I just wanted to forget. To disconnect from the world, the then-new war in Ukraine, what toxic know-nothing was going to win a congressional seat in what state, the floods, the fires, the shootings, how much money I was losing in the stock market. It wasn't that I didn't care. It was that I was exhausted from caring. And maybe, you know, I just wanted to be plain old exhausted. Bone tired. Every ounce of energy expended at the end of the day. I was perched at a place of privilege where I could choose the hard stuff, where purposeful, self-imposed "suffering" was an adventure.

Maybe I was frightened that I, like everyone else, had grown used to calling this the "new normal" and going about my business, so accustomed to the storm, the shitstorm, that we didn't know any other weather. Maybe I just didn't want to sit at home and wait for the next shitstorm. Maybe I was tired of being battered. Maybe I was appalled to learn that the 2022 word of the year was *permacrisis*.

After all of this, after what we'd seen and lived through—and not *after* but *now, during, in real time*—the nastiness and erosion of faith, the diminution of hope, the absence of charity, I wondered, *What shape are we in? What shape am I in?* On the Camino, I would test the physical, push my body to do this hard thing, to walk up steep hills and down rocky slot canyons, to walk in sheeting rain and howling wind, to walk seven, eight, nine hours a day and wake up and do it again the next day and the next after that. I knew about tests like this. I had put my body through physical rigors for the joy of it, for the challenge. But this was about assessing my emotional shape, spiritual shape, psychological shape. It was about finding a way to understand loss, to acknowledge wounds, to make peace with the past, to find an authentic path forward into the rest of my life. Hell, to think there was a "rest of my life." I needed to answer the question so very many of us face at a time of loss or upheaval, transition or disconnect: *What now?*

1

DAY TWO ON THE Camino, and I knew nothing. I had yet to learn that I carried too much water and not enough food, that the revered "Brierley"—the guidebook everyone used—could be full of shit, that the trail would be kinder and crueler than I ever imagined, that, among the scores of fellow hikers I randomly encountered, I would meet *una amiga de mi alma*. Also: I didn't know if I could do this thing. I didn't know, now that I was here, now that I had talked myself into this, now that I had boldly and publicly announced my intentions, if I *wanted* to do this thing. Friends told me I was "brave." I didn't feel brave. I felt anxious. I wasn't worried about my physical strength, about my ability to walk almost five hundred miles. I took my body for granted. I was worried about my lifelong inability to just let things happen, to go with the flow. I was a planner. But planning had not worked out so well lately. Yes, I planned. *We* planned. John Lennon had said it first, back fifty years ago when it was not yet a cliché, a meme, or a bumper sticker: "Life is what happens when you're busy making other plans." And so life happened. Or, more to the point: Death happened.

I was trying to extract every little lesson I could from this past year because learning lessons is how I figured I could stand grief on its head. The Lennon-inspired mantra for me was this: Don't bank on a future that may never happen. Don't live in a future that may never happen. Planning doesn't make things happen. And meanwhile, I told myself, I *lectured* to myself: Loosen up. Open up. Allow what happens to happen, not in an *ob-la-di, ob-la-da* way—I cannot do *ob-la-di, ob-la-da*—but from a gentler space that I would like to learn to inhabit. The learning-to-inhabit was going to be way harder than the walking. I knew that, which was why I was on edge. On day two, I still felt very much the pilgrim impostor with my too-big backpack and my new hiking poles, calling out the hearty *buen camino* greeting I now knew was expected when I encountered a fellow walker.

Two days before, I had awoken in a strange room in a narrow, hard bed in an *albergue*—a new word for me, the adult version of a youth hostel—in Saint-Jean-Pied-de-Port. It was not easy to get to this point of departure for the Camino Francés. For me, it involved three airports, two planes, a bus, a shuttle, and a walk. And when I started this, I was already in Europe. When I finally arrived, hefting that backpack that I already knew was too heavy, I thought, *Well, the hard part is over*. This, of course, was a laughably clueless thought. But I admit that I savored it for a moment.

The heart of town was a steep, cobblestoned street lined with albergues. There was also a small but extraordinarily well-stocked "pilgrims' store," where I bought lightweight hiking poles, and the official pilgrims' office, where I stood in line to get my Credencial del Peregrino. Or in my case, *peregrina* (the feminine of the Spanish word for pilgrim). It is kind of a passport. Every day you walk, you get the credencial stamped to show your progress. Albergues, churches, coffee shops, and restaurants that cater to pilgrims all have special stamps—*sellos*—they use. At the end of this trek (a day that was beyond my imagination), I could take my fully stamped credencial to another official pilgrims' office, this one hundreds of miles and more than a month away, in Santiago. There I will receive my *compostela*, my certificate of completion. Santiago, the city in northwestern Spain, the terminus for all the official Caminos, is actually named Santiago de Compostela for just this reason.

And so that afternoon, I bought my poles and picked up my credencial while receiving a long lecture from an elderly British mansplainer, a Camino veteran now volunteering at the office, about blisters, dehydration, bedbugs, and not leaving toilet paper on the trail. Then I made my way up the street to my albergue, where I sat on my cot (which I carefully inspected for bedbugs) and spread the entire contents of my backpack on the floor in front of me, staring at the array, wishing I knew what I didn't need so I could get rid of it now. I also wished, for a brief, lonely, self-pitying moment, that I had a partner with me to do this. Whatever *this* was. It was an irrational thought, as self-pitying ones often are, because one of the points of this journey was to be alone, to learn *how* to be alone after being coupled for my entire adult life. Even as I teared up, I also thought, *Who in the world would you actually want as a companion?* Tom would never, ever have joined me. This trek, with its physical exertion and rustic accommodations, would be his idea of a really bad time. He and Lizzie, our daughter, were of a single mind about adventures like this: No way. My sons were partnered, employed, and busy with their lives. My friends? I wanted to keep them as friends. A trek like this might deepen a friendship, but it also might ruin it. I wouldn't want to take the risk.

Sitting on the hard, narrow bed, staring at my stuff on the floor, I also wished that this journey, whatever it was going to be, was already over and done with. Then I beat myself up for being wimpy. Then I beat myself up for beating myself up. Then I went for a walk down the cobblestone street. Over a little bridge, I located the very first Camino way marker, a bright yellow arrow.

The guidebook stated that tomorrow's trek, from this quaint little French town to the Spanish village of Roncesvalles, would be about twenty-four kilometers. I knew Roncesvalles would be my first stop because there was nothing in between here and there except for a tiny hostel nestled in the Pyrenees. It was necessary to reserve a space in this hostel many months in advance. I had not done that, a maiden attempt to *just let it happen*.

The guidebook told me it would take seven to nine hours of walking to reach Roncesvalles. That would be more walking than I had ever done in a single day. I stopped reading.

I didn't want to know any more than I already did. I would wake up and walk. That's it. I repacked my pack, eliminating nothing, and then settled in for a short, fitful night's sleep. Would it have been shorter and more fitful had I known what I would learn that next day—that the first 19 kilometers of the trek over the Pyrenees would involve an elevation gain of 1,350 meters (that's 4,700 feet) and the next 5 kilometers would be a killer 1,500-foot descent? That there would be no switchbacks, just straight up, straight down?

Now, at the end of day two, I found myself in Larrasoaña, an eight-hundred-plus-year-old village in the northern Spanish province of Navarre. I had walked thirty-five miles in two days, two very long days. Although I would mostly stop thinking like this later, because it would cease to make any sense or be mildly amusing or help me in any way, I considered that this same distance, which took me sixteen hours to walk, would have taken me a half hour to drive. I approached the town, found my way across a lovely stone bridge—the plaque said *Puente de los Bandidos*—and down a narrow lane to an albergue that I had chosen the night before, courtesy of one of the three pilgrim apps I had downloaded on my phone. The host directed me to a room on the second floor with four sets of metal bunk beds that would eventually be inhabited by eight people, all women. I thought same-sex rooms were the usual thing in albergues. I didn't know this would never happen again. We women shared a bathroom, which was clean and had a new bar of soap and a tiled shower with abundant hot water. I thought this was the usual thing. I didn't know this would never happen again. I took a shower. A shower at the end of a long day, even—as I was to learn—a bad shower, a shower where you had to press a button every fifteen seconds to keep the water coming out, a shower that smelled of mold and feet, even that kind of shower, was a wonderment. This shower was that and more.

Back in the small room, I tucked myself into the bottom bunk below Michele from Quebec, who was busy writing in her journal (which it occurred to me I should be doing, but I hadn't brought a notebook, in a wrongheaded attempt to save backpack weight) and across from Margit from Sweden, who was bandaging her already blistered toes. In this roomful of women—not one of whom snored—I fell asleep easily. This would not happen again. Neither the nonsnoring nor the falling-asleep-easily, the connection being obvious.

That night, I had a dream so real, so palpable, that when I awoke, I was convinced it had actually happened. In the dream, Tom knelt beside the bunk bed, reached in, and touched my shoulder. I *felt* that touch. In the dream, I got out of bed. I stood up. And we embraced, the kind of full-body embrace that lasts long enough for you to feel the other person's body heat. I felt that embrace. I *felt* that heat. Then we stood apart.

"Go," he said.

When you dream, your subconscious is trying to tell you something. When you dream of people who have died, you pay close attention.

"Go," said Tom, who had been for three decades my husband.

It was a command, both forceful and loving. But it was also, or so it seemed to me when I awoke in the dark the next morning, him giving me permission. Not permission to do this thing—I didn't need that from him, dead or alive—but permission to walk into a future that did not include him. Permission to become who I was going to become.

2

TOM WAS NOT THE first man I lived with, not the first man to whom I said *I love you*. But he was The One. The others, the two others, were practice for him, the warm-up acts. Because what do you know when you are eighteen or twenty-four? What do you know about who you are and what you want? P was sophisticated and urbane, or so it seemed to a girl from the potato fields of Long Island. He was deeply and interestingly neurotic. Until he wasn't. Interesting, that is. He remained neurotic. B was his opposite: the sunniest, most carefree person I had ever met. Carefree was such a relief, until it wasn't. Until there were actually things to care about. At the beginning, Tom was whom I needed, then he was whom I wanted. Then he was who was there. Maybe that's the way long marriages go.

Do I start from the end and go backward? Yes, I think I do, because to know Tom is to know how he died.

The EOL package arrives by special messenger on September 24. *EOL* stands for *End of Life*. In Oregon, and in nine other states and the District of Columbia, the terminally ill have the legal right to end their lives on their own terms. Oregon was the first, back almost thirty years ago, to enact this legislation. It was a tough fight, with pushback from doctors, who interpreted the "first, do no harm" Hippocratic oath as meaning don't in any way aid in someone's dying, and religious folks who believed death was in God's hands. There were some who believed the right to die would be overused and abused, perhaps by the deeply depressed, perhaps—and this was the ugliest of arguments—by younger family members "forcing" older family members to end their lives to either save on medical bills or hasten their inheritance.

The law passed. Tom and I were both enthusiastic supporters. We talked about how we would choose this way to end our lives. We were young and healthy with three little kids, and it was all theoretical. Who imagines death when it seems so far away as not to exist at all? The law passed both because people saw the goodness and kindness of it—many pointed out that we allow our ailing animals this dignity—but also because of all the rules and regulations, the safeguards and fail-safes. There were all kinds of stipulations, hoops one had to jump through, specific diagnoses that qualified, oral and written requests, multiple documents and forms to sign, waiting periods to observe, witnesses to certify, physicians to see, interviews with well-meaning hospice volunteers, calls from well-meaning social workers, more waiting periods, checklists. But in the end, it was just the person deciding this is the way to exit. It was just the person opening the EOL package. The year Tom died, 383 people requested EOL medications; 219 used them.

The package arrives. It's here at the house, but I don't want Tom to open it. What is in this package makes possible what will happen. What is in this package makes it official. This is the next-to-final step. It is no longer about thinking and planning and talking. It is about doing.

He opens the small box, spreads out the pages of instructions on the bed, inspects the little bottles containing the medications, reads, falls asleep reading. He sleeps a lot. I sit on the couch by his bed and watch him. I sit and watch him a lot. A few minutes later, his ragged breathing awakens him. The tumor, the biggest one in his right lung, the one that grew even as he went through rounds of chemo, prevents him from taking a deep breath. Even, sometimes, a shallow breath. He is awake, and he looks exactly like himself, except his hair never came back fully from the chemo. But he never had good hair anyway. His beard came back, though. He has always, since the day I met him, sported a beard. He's wearing one of the many Eddie Bauer flannel shirts I've bought him. His color is not bad. His eyes are clear. If you didn't know better, you would, in that moment, never think you were looking at a man with an incurable, untreatable disease. He finds his breath. He looks at me. "I've had enough," he says. "I'm done."

And yet, he is not quite done. His physician has prescribed oxycodone for "pain related to cancer." I don't know about the prescription, which Tom must have asked for, or the pain, which he does not talk about, until many months later when I go over his medical file. But the EOL package sits on the mantel for three weeks. Tom spends the days sleeping, dozing on a deck chair on the porch, reading Lao Tzu. Most days, he finds the energy to get dressed. Most days, he eats. He develops an odd craving for Coke Zero. I buy six-packs at the store every other day. He doesn't want to talk to anyone. Except me. It is hard for him to speak more than a sentence without succumbing to what is called *paroxysmal* coughing, intermittent attacks of uncontrollable, violent coughing that can feel exhausting and painful. But he has the strength and endurance of a six-foot-tall, two-hundred-pound, mid-sixties male body that he has mostly treated quite well through the years. If he were not to take his death under his control, he could probably live like this—coughing, breathless, enervated—for many months. Too many, he thinks. And I understand.

He chooses a day, October 15. The night before, our last night together, there is no ritualizing, no soul-baring, no rending of garments. We've already done that. Except for the garment thing. We watch an episode of *Modern Family* sitting propped up on pillows side by side on the narrow hospital bed I had delivered two weeks ago when Tom could no longer walk up the stairs to our bedroom. I rearranged the living room, placing the bed between the fireplace, the couch, and the media cabinet, removing the ugly institutional rubber mattress protector and replacing it with our own soft bed linens. We started rewatching the series months ago, beginning with the final season and then going backward. We're on season 3 now. We won't make it to the end because tomorrow Tom is going to die.

I give him a chaste kiss, quickly, closed mouth, because his strangled breathing makes anything else impossible. Then I go upstairs to sleep in one of the kids' old bedrooms. I haven't slept in our bedroom for months. Sleeping together before he moved to the hospital bed downstairs was difficult for both of us. He coughed himself awake six, seven, eight times a night, a raspy, insistent cough that robbed him of breath. A few times, this caused him to lose consciousness. It's called *tussive syncope*. I looked it up because it scared the hell out of me. Tom looked it up because he researched everything about this disease and probably knew more than his oncologist. The first time he fainted, which is what syncope is, he stopped breathing, and his eyes rolled back in his head. I thought he had died.

In our bed at night, I would fall into a shallow sleep waiting for the cough. From time to time, and then more often than not, I would quietly leave the bed when he fell back to sleep, walking down the hall to the room that used to be our eldest son's. Tom encouraged me to sleep the whole night there. He said knowing that his cough was going to awaken me just increased his anxiety. And so, I begin to sleep in that room every night. When he moves downstairs, I don't move back into our bedroom. It doesn't feel right to sleep there without him.

That morning, I am awake at 4:30. I feel the cool air from the open window behind my head. I do not hear a cough. I think, *Tomorrow when I wake up, it will be to a world without him.*

The day is beautiful: brilliant sun, cloudless sky, almost a peacock blue, autumn leaves aflame. While Tom cycles in and out of sleep in the hospital bed in the living room, our sons and

I take a three-mile walk down a country lane. Our daughter is on her way to us. She lives in a little coastal town several hours away. The boys and I walk, passing no one. We talk easily, as we always have. Mothers and sons can do that. Often mothers and daughters cannot. We don't talk about what is happening or what is going to happen. We don't trade memories. We talk about the garden and how now that it's mid-October, it's time to put it to bed. We talk about what we will cook for dinner. But mostly we don't talk. We walk, we breathe, we reach out to one another, every once in a while, to grab a hand, touch a shoulder.

At home, Tom is sitting up in bed in his big gray fleece bathrobe, the one I bought him so many years ago that has become, like the Velveteen Rabbit, real. It's late afternoon when our daughter arrives. Tom rouses himself—what an effort this must be now—and moves to sit on an oversize chair in the corner of the room. Our daughter sits at his feet, her hand resting on his knee. I want to take a picture of this, but of course I don't. The moment is theirs. There is so much to talk about and so little breath. I do not listen in—I go into the kitchen to make dinner—but I know what he is saying. He is telling her what he has been telling her since we learned about the life she had been living, four years ago, or was it longer? He is telling her that he loves her, that he believes in her, that she is capable of so much more. I have a copy of a letter he sent to her after she was beaten by the man she had chosen to be her boyfriend, the man she said she loved, the man who said he'd never do it again, the man who did it again.

He wrote:

> I love you with all my heart. So it breaks my heart when I see you losing your life, your health, and

> your self-respect. I think you had great hopes of helping FA. Instead, he is dragging you down. Mom and I don't love your relationship with FA—it is bad and getting worse. We don't love your meth addiction. It is bad, too. But we love you—very, very much. You know, because we have talked about this so many times, that we are here when you are ready. We are here. We love you.

I think Tom thought, I *know* he thought, that this literal deathbed talk would be what turned the tables. When I came back into the room, my daughter's head was resting on my husband's thigh.

No one wants to eat. I knew that when I was making dinner. It just gave me something to do. Tom makes his way, slowly, across the room back to the bed. He sits on the edge, hands on his knees, bent over, coughing. Then he straightens up, reaches for a glass of water, and takes the first two pills, the pre-meds that were part of the EOL package. These are antianxiety pills, Valium or Xanax or something like that. He leans back on the pillows. I don't know this until it happens, but Tom has instructed Jackson, our older son, in how to perform an energy-clearing ceremony using Tom's mesa—a ritual bundle of stones collected during his trips with shamanic healers. Those trips, his interest in shamanism, had been surprising—and quite wonderful—to me. He was a science guy. There was nothing woo-woo about him. And yet there was this, his interest in Q'ero-Peruvian spirituality, in accessing what is not visible but is palpable. Our son places the mesa on Tom's lap and walks slowly around the room, waving a vulture feather in the air. Something is happening. I don't know what. But it is powerful.

Our son completes the circuit. Tom closes his eyes. "I need a moment," he says. We all leave the room. When we come back, we position ourselves around the bed as if we have planned this, but we haven't. I mix the medications for him, the "cocktail." The first will put him to sleep and then into unconsciousness. This will happen quickly. The second will stop his heart. The instructions say this could take anywhere from ten minutes to an hour. He wraps his hand around the scarred jelly jar I used. He has more to say.

He tells us, in his best science-lecture voice—one I have heard so often these past decades, the one that alternately impresses and annoys me—that he is energy, that we are all energy, and that energy can neither be created nor destroyed. "I will be out there," he tells us. "Use me," he says. "Use me to power your lives." Even as I am a captive of this moment, I am also an observer, marveling at his grace, at the gift he is giving us. He smiles. Is it possible that he smiles? Am I remembering this correctly? Yes, he smiles. The jelly jar is in his hands. The instructions warn that the liquid is biting, bitter, distasteful. Our daughter has placed a jar of honey and a little spoon on the bedside table. Tom takes a spoonful, then quickly downs the liquid through a straw.

"I'm going on a great journey," he says, leaning back. "I'll see you later."

The American experience with death, that final scene, most often takes place in a hospital room with machines and tubes and strangers, with the person dying having lost control over how and where and when they die, with loved ones either standing vigil by the bedside watching the monitors to see, on-screen, when the body quits, or loved ones rushed to the hospital in time to witness the end. There is sudden death, the wallop of that, and there is the slow, painful—emphasis on the painful—descent into frailty and decrepitude and pain and then the half-life of morphine drips. The weight of that. The grinding grief of that. That is not this. This is sacred. This is, if such a word can be used to describe the death of the person you have made a life with for so long that you can barely remember another life, beautiful.

Sleep comes quickly, and then it deepens. His breathing slows, and although it is not easy breathing, neither is he coughing. *He is not coughing.* The gift of that. We all are holding on to a piece of him, an arm, a leg, a foot. I hold his hand, his right hand. It is warm, and the fingers remain curled around mine even as his sleep deepens into unconsciousness. Or maybe I am misremembering that. Maybe it is my fingers that are holding tight and his that have loosened. There is spittle in the corner of his mouth, and I use my other hand to grab a tissue and wipe his lips. He breathes. We breathe. We wait. That cliché, "time stands still"? That is this. And yet, of course, time passes. Ten minutes, fifteen, thirty. A few times his breathing stops, and we all look up at one another from our sentinel posts around him, and then his breathing begins again. Slower this time.

I have read about agonal breathing, a sign that a person is near death. I want to be prepared, if there is such a thing as being prepared to watch someone die. I think the shock will be softened if I know what to expect. This is delusional. But sometimes delusional is just what you need. This end-of-life breathing, my internet sources have told me, is often labored and noisy. There can be gasping, moaning, and groaning. It makes sense, doesn't it, that we exit life mirroring how we entered it, how our mothers breathed and labored. I think none of this at the moment. I think nothing. I only listen and wait. We wait. Tom continues to breathe, slower and slower and shallower and shallower. No gasps, no moaning, just quieter and quieter. And then nothing.

A friend, Jonas, who is an ER doctor, has been sitting in Tom's office, detached from the house, all this time. The death-with-dignity, end-of-life-care hospice volunteers, all those well-meaning folks who have cycled in and out of our lives these past few months, have suggested we have someone "experienced" there with us. We talked about this, our sons and I, Tom and I, and we agreed that we did not want a stranger here. We have known this newly minted doctor since he was in middle school, his family and our family intertwined the way parents do when their kids are best friends. My younger son, Zane, goes out to get him. Jonas stands over Tom, Tom's body, and places his stethoscope, gently, moving it from place to place, listening for a long time. "He's gone," he tells us.

After a while, Zane steps out to the porch and calls the mortuary. After a while, two men come with a gurney. One of them says, "Maybe you don't want to watch this part." None of us is going to leave this room. We watch as the men lift Tom's body from the hospital bed and place it on the gurney. They start to cover his face, and I tell them no.

A few years before, Tom and I had engaged in lengthy and heated discussions about selling this house, buying another piece of land, and building a new house. I was in favor. I was more than "in favor." I really wanted to do this. It's not that I always got my way, but often if I made a persuasive case, tirelessly, I wore him down. Tom could not be budged. "The only way I'm leaving this house," he told me, "is feetfirst."

The men wheel him out, feetfirst. I tell the kids what their father said. The trite thing to say is, "We laughed so hard we cried." But we were crying already. And then we were laughing. And then the hearse drove away.

3

THIS DAY, MY THIRD day on the Camino, was supposed to be an easy one. I had walked 25 kilometers over the Pyrenees on my first day. Starting at dawn, fueled by anxiety and wonder, I had made it over the mountains, supposedly the hardest hike of the entire Camino Francés. (This, by the way—and spoiler alert—was not true.) On the second day, I had walked 27.4 kilometers—6 kilometers longer than the recommended stop—because I wanted to avoid replicating the prescribed "stages" in the Camino guidebook everyone was using. I thought if I stopped where others stopped, finding accommodations for the night might be harder. Also, I didn't want to be part of some loose pilgrim grouping that had started the journey in Saint-Jean when I did, and stopped for café con leches at the same places, and hunkered down for the night in the same albergues. Many hikers, I was to learn, cherished this camaraderie, this instant kinship. People thought—and later blogged—about the folks they encountered on the trail as their "Camino family." I had just lost two-fifths of my family. *Family* meant something entirely different to me.

On that extra six-kilometer stretch into the next village, I saw no one at all on the narrow path that snaked through beech and pine forests, the midafternoon sun hidden behind a wall of trees. I was on edge and on the alert, *hyperalert*, for Camino way markers—those painted yellow arrows pointing the way. They periodically, if only temporarily, reassured me that I was on the right path and would eventually arrive at the next village. Six kilometers is less than four miles, but I'd already walked thirteen miles that day, and the solitude of that path, the darkening afternoon, was unnerving. It was the solitude I craved and had actively chosen. But that late afternoon, I had second thoughts.

I am a terrible singer. My father once (or twice or far more often than that) remarked that I "carried a tune on my back." On that lonely stretch, I sang aloud and loudly, alternating between the Stones' "You Can't Always Get What You Want" and a long-ago Girl Scout song so deeply embedded in my brain that I remembered all the lyrics:

I'm happy when I'm hiking, pack upon my back.
I'm happy when I'm hiking, off the beaten track.
Out in the open country, that's the place for me.
With a right good friend to the journey's end,
Ten, twenty, thirty, forty, fifty miles a day.

I was decidedly not "happy" with the pack upon my back. And I did not have a "right good friend," but the sound of my own out-of-tune voice kept me company and kept me going.

That morning, buoyed by the dream—*Go,* Tom had said—fresh from a good night's sleep, optimistic about the 16.5-kilometer day ahead, the shortest distance so far, I set out on the path to Pamplona. I had a plan to meet up with a woman I had encountered on the afternoon of that brutal first day. I wasn't looking for a friend, I wasn't looking for a Camino sister, but Kiki and I fell in with each other as we sucked air and cursed at the relentless uphill climb over the Pyrenees. Our breath may have been labored, but our conversation was anything but. Almost immediately—and I do not remember how this happened—we started talking about the work of the writer Geraldine Brooks. How often does one randomly encounter, trudging up a mountain, leaning into an endless ascent, a stranger who can discuss the extraordinary archival research undertaken by a fiction writer? We moved on to Joan Didion and Margaret Atwood. A Mary Oliver poem may have been mentioned. And quoted. The breathing-hard conversation was casual and relaxed, while also being sparky and surprising. I loved that we didn't trade personal information beyond the basic name, rank, and serial number. I very much wanted to keep my wounds, which is to say my backstory, hidden. To have someone look at me without pity or concern, to know that a person was not struggling to figure out what to say—this was truly liberating.

Kiki had stopped in Zubiri, the village I passed by on the way to Larrasoaña. This next day, this third day, I am ahead of her by several miles, but I am looking forward to finding her in Pamplona. The walk is through oak forests, over stone bridges, through a series of small villages, and then descending into the city. It is on this easy-mileage day I discover that my oh-so-carefully planned and curated and angsted-over "lightweight" pack proves itself to be unbearable. The more-than-bothersome, less-than-life-threatening ache I feel, step by step, all day, has resulted in self-talk that goes like this:

> *Everything you put in that backpack was carefully selected. Every item is lightweight, featherweight, even. You carefully considered grams and ounces. You chose that rain jacket you didn't like because it weighed 3 ounces less than the one you did like. You bought that expensive ultralight sleeping bag that closes with little plastic snaps because this zipperless version is 2.2 ounces lighter. You parceled out three Band-Aids for the first aid kit instead of including a box. You invested in toothpaste tablets rather than a tube. You didn't bring a notebook. And yet: The backpack is too heavy.*

Because everything weighs something.

This becomes a mantra. And, kilometer after kilometer, the mantra opens up to bigger thoughts, not about the weight of that damned 45L Osprey but about those other "little" things that we believe won't weigh on us, so we pay them no mind, we stuff them in our backpacks and keep on going. That harsh remark, that misunderstanding that was never cleared up, that time someone disappointed us, that time we disappointed someone, that thing we said that we wish we hadn't, that thing we didn't say that we wish we had, that time we needed help and didn't get it, that time we didn't give help when it was needed. All those times. The little stuff. The lightweight stuff that adds up.

Because everything weighs something.

My particular baggage is not featherweight. At this moment in my life, I find that I am burdened with heavier items. How ironic that to lose the living, breathing, warm weight of a husband and a daughter, that absence weighs so much. There is a heft to grief—the obesity of grief, as memoirist Lynn Haraldson called it—that cannot be explained or therapized (or written) away. It must be borne. Like the damned backpack.

The shoulder straps, which I learn much later are especially constructed as narrower and thinner on this model to lessen the weight of the pack itself, dig into my unusually bony clavicle. The constant and direct pressure is surprisingly painful. I stop to adjust the straps. I take off the pack, extricate my puffer jacket, and wrap the sleeves around the straps. This relieves the pressure for maybe ten minutes. I stop in front of a little church in one of the villages, sit on a stone wall, and gingerly remove the pack and the puffer. I am apparently wincing.

A woman walks out of the church, a fellow pilgrim, small and slender, sixtyish. She sits next to me on the stone wall and asks if I'm okay. I manage a smile, tell her I'm fine. But meanwhile, I'm massaging my now angry-red collarbone. She reaches into her pack, rummages around, and comes up with a piece of sheepskin. She hasn't said a word. She pulls my pack toward her and wraps the sheepskin around the strap that's causing the injury. "Try that," she says. Her name is Emily. She is a teacher from Australia. I heft the pack back onto my shoulders, and the sheepskin helps. This is a real "random act of kindness." I am almost teary when I thank her.

We walk together for a while, mostly silently. She has a lightness to her, which makes the silence comfortable. After a half hour, I do not want to tell her that the sheepskin has ceased doing its work. The pain is back. We part ways as we approach Pamplona. She is in search of her companions, who went ahead while she helped me at the church. I am in search of Kiki.

It is right then, following the Camino markers into the old walled part of the city, that I discover that my "international plan" from Verizon is not working. I did not download a map I could use offline, part of my plan to not plan. And so I am map-less. On the trail, this matters very little. In fact, I had not tried to connect on the trail. There are Camino way markers to guide us pilgrims. Walking through small villages, a map is not needed either. Often the Camino is the main street—*calle mayor*—and the path is straight through. But Pamplona is different. Pamplona is a city of two hundred thousand that must be navigated. I have an address for my accommodations tonight but absolutely no idea where the place might be. The path wraps around a section of the medieval wall that was built to protect the city, and then, all of a sudden, I am on a narrow street jammed with people, a crush of people, a throng, a horde. I am immediately sucked into the vortex. The crowds are so thick that I cannot see anything other than the shoulders and backs of the people in front of me. I am being jostled—and jostling. Every time somebody bumps against me, my pack shifts, and the shoulder strap presses into my bone.

For long minutes, fifteen or twenty, the crowd in the street does not move, and neither do I. If this sounds claustrophobic and suffocating: Yes. Hours later when we are sampling tapas at an out-door bar, Kiki tells me that this day, September 25, is set aside to celebrate Saint Fermín, a legendary holy man, the first bishop of

Pamplona, the co–patron saint of the province of Navarre. Persecuted and beheaded (apparently not uncommon in the third century), he was later sanctified based on the miracles that allegedly followed his death. The sweet odor that arose from his grave was credited with causing ice and snow to melt, bringing about the blooming of flowers, the bending of nearby trees toward his grave site, and a miraculous spring. Also, icing on the cake, the sick were cured. Kiki apparently knows everything there is to know.

I know none of this wedged in the street crowd. But I catch on pretty quickly that this is a very big, very loud party. It also begins to occur to me, with my backpack full of what feels like rocks, and my bone bruise, and my utter ignorance about where I am headed, that I am perhaps not as invincible as I tell myself I am, as I must tell myself I am to do what I am doing. This thought will reoccur—and I will beat it back—scores of times during the weeks to follow. It is my cloak of invincibility. It is both necessary and harmful.

The ass-to-elbow crowd begins to move ever so slowly. I make it to an intersection, turn onto a somewhat less packed little street, duck into a doorway, and start asking everyone who passes, "*¿Dónde está . . . ?*," showing them the accommodations and address on my phone. Most people shrug; some people—revelers—just ignore me. No one knows. I walk on. People are dancing in the street. There are musicians and singers on every corner. Parades pass by with marchers on stilts. I know this is magical and amazing, and yet all I want to do is find the little hotel and take off the backpack.

Instead, I find a deserted plaza tucked behind an alley, sit on a low stone wall, lean my back against the base of a statue. A stooped and gnarled old woman hobbles by using a cane. This is like a scene out of the Brothers Grimm.

"*¿Por que lloras?*" *Why are you crying?* she asks. My Spanish is not good, but it is good enough. I didn't realize I was crying. I tell her I am lost and ask about the hotel. She pats my hand and takes it in hers, and we walk there together. The place is just on the other side of the little alley I had turned down, less than fifty meters away. I cannot repay this kindness. I will never see this woman again. She will never know that I will someday write about her.

There are more surprises in store. The little hotel cannot find my reservation, and they are full up for the night. But the woman behind the desk takes pity on me—I do, in fact, present as pitiful—and finds me a windowless cubby the size of a prison cell, with a twin bed wedged against the wall and barely enough room to open the door. But the bed has two pillows. Two! And sheets. And a telephone-booth-size private bathroom. With towels. Although I have spent only three nights in "rustic" accommodations without such—or any—luxuries, it seems like much longer. This cubby feels palatial to me. I drop my pack, unlace my walking shoes, flop on the bed, and vow never to take the comfort of my life for granted ever again. (It is a vow I manage to keep for perhaps four days after I return home to my life of comfort.) I rinse out my socks in the washbasin the size of a cereal bowl, slip my feet into flip-flops, and climb the stairs to Kiki's room, where we get drunk on cheap wine sloshed into plastic cups before we head back out into the crowds.

4

I WALK SOUTHWEST OUT of Pamplona in the early-morning darkness, glad to leave the noise and the people behind. Kiki will stay another day. We will meet up later down the road, we tell each other. Camino way markers are not as easy to spot on city streets as they are in villages or along the trail, and so almost as soon as I set off, I am lost. It is too early in the day to feel anxious, but I do. I backtrack down a side street, search for an arrow marker, see nothing, start down another street that I think might be the right direction. No signs. No other hikers with backpacks. No one on the street at all.

The sky begins to lighten behind me, pink and yellow and pastel blue. Over my right shoulder, I see a faint rainbow. *Yes, I am truly lost, but really*, I tell myself, *is this so bad?* Maybe a minute after this thought occurs to me, I see a faded yellow arrow painted on the side of a building. I was lost; now I am not. The timing feels magical because I need it to feel magical. It also feels contrived, like if someone told me this happened—this Zen-like moment of letting go and then, boom, receiving—I would groan.

This is obviously a teaching moment. It seems my days are now filled with these. In fact, this journey is beginning to feel like one long teaching moment. I mostly love this, but then I don't. Does everything have to be a goddamned teaching moment? Can't I just disappear into the experience and stop trying to mine it for insights, to extract lessons? Why does everything have to mean something? Can't I just walk? Apparently not.

Today's lesson is not over yet. The sun is up. And now I am seeing signs every kilometer or so, signs that unmistakably point me in the right direction: yellow arrows on the sides of barns, on fences, on stone walls, on utility poles; newer turquoise-blue signs with canary-yellow clamshells. Sometimes these signs are eye level and hard to miss. Sometimes they are faded, barely visible. I know that I can go a long way without seeing a sign, and I know what it feels like to move from concern to worry to mild panic when I don't. I also know that sense of relief that almost borders on exaltation when I finally do see a sign. And I think: *I wish life were like the Camino, and every so often, just when you needed it, there is a sign to tell you, to reassure you, that you are on the right path.* And then I think: *Maybe life* is *like this, but we just don't see the signs that are right in front of us, or we see them and ignore them, or we are just looking elsewhere.* And then I think: *Why do we need signs anyway? Why don't we trust our, as the self-helpers say, "inner compass"?* And then I think: *Stop thinking. Just walk.*

That lasts for half a minute, maybe less. The thing about a well-trained, intricately wired monkey mind (mine) is you can't order it to stop. I keep thinking about the idea of signs and the need to be reassured. A few mornings ago, walking in the moonless dark of 6:00 a.m., seeing no signs after I left a little village, I see in the distance the dim yellow light of a headlamp, of a person walking way ahead of me on the road. Although I probably won't catch up—in fact, I don't want to catch up—I feel gratitude and friendship for this person I don't know. And I think of that E. L. Doctorow quote I am so fond of: "Writing is like driving at night in the fog. You can only see as far as your headlights, but you can make the whole trip that way." And that, really, is how I am making my way: from sign to sign, by the light of my headlamp, by the light of the headlamps of those ahead of me.

It turns out to be a tough day. There's a long, slow ascent past crumbling monasteries and vast stretches of hayfields, now, this being late September, stubbled and tawny. Then the trail becomes a steep, loose-graveled climb to one of the most photographed spots on the Camino Francés, Alto de Perdón, which translates as the Hill of Forgiveness. The "hill" is 2,460 feet high. At the top of this windy peak, with a view of massive wind turbines to the left and the agricultural valley below, sits a long metal sculpture, a larger-than-life parade of pilgrims on foot and on horseback. There is a Spanish inscription on it, *Dónde se cruza el camino del viento con el de las estrellas*, meaning, "Where the path of the wind crosses that of the stars."

The wind is close to gale force, or so it seems to me, and to those spinning turbines on the nearby ridge. I am far from alone up here. In addition to four or five small clusters of fellow pilgrims resting from the climb, chugging water, downing snacks, and posing themselves in front of the sculpture, there is a group of Guardia Civil officers. Along with the National Police, they are in charge of keeping the Camino safe. And it is. The safety of the Camino, the liberating thought that I could walk alone and not be scared, is one of the reasons I chose this long journey instead of others in my own much-less-safe country.

The officers are all young and handsome. They are smiling and laughing and look like they're readying for a *GQ* photo shoot. They offer to take photos of pilgrims in front of the statues. They say yes to selfies. This is an odd and beautiful scene: the statues that honor the thousand-year history of the Camino, the thirty-story-high turbines on the ridge, the ragtag pilgrims with their dusty boots and backpacks, the fashionable Guardia, the whipping wind. I, too, drink water, eat a power bar, take a selfie, and then move on.

The descent is far more challenging than the climb. It takes most of the afternoon to navigate the close-to-tortuous rocky plunge down into the valley. When you have to concentrate so hard, when so much of your attention is focused on where to step and where to place your poles and how not to fall, this can be scary. But I am not scared. It's not that I am brave. It is that, despite all evidence to the contrary, I continue to believe that I am (almost) invulnerable. Physically, at least. Also, this kind of grit-your-teeth, sweaty effort scours my mind. This is about as close as I get to a meditative state.

I end this day as I began it, getting lost. Worn out from the hike, nursing that bruise on my collarbone, I wander the winding cobblestone streets of an ancient town I know I would appreciate more if I could just find my albergue. And of course, eventually, I do. And then, relieved of my pack, my feet happy in flip-flops, I wander the streets again in search of a place to eat dinner. I find a small café hidden away on a narrow side street. There, sitting at a table with her two walking companions, is Emily, the Australian woman I haven't seen since she tried to help alleviate my backpack problems a few days ago. We had spent perhaps an hour together then. We hug like old friends.

I lose her the next day as I walk through olive orchards and vineyards, through a series of small villages, down more narrow, winding streets, in and out of tiny cafés to refuel with café con leche. And then, a day later, we find each other on the approach to yet another sleepy little town. It had been raining, misting really, all morning, and the cobblestone streets are slick. We turn a corner and see a small group gathered around a man sitting on the ground. When we get closer, we see that his forehead is bleeding, and he has a big, ugly gash across his nose. His left leg is outstretched, elevated on a backpack. That foot is shoeless and sockless. The ankle is wrapped. His toes are swollen and blue. We learn that he had slipped and fallen a few minutes before. Brian, a nurse from Colorado whom I had met and walked with briefly the day before, had wrapped the ankle.

Others walk with first aid kits, a few Band-Aids, a packet of antiseptic wipes, a tube of antibiotic ointment. Brian walks with a full medical kit, with the supplies necessary to treat a serious injury. And that's what he is doing there on the wet stones, kneeling by the man. Another pilgrim whose phone has a Spanish SIM card had just called an ambulance. It will take a while to get here. A third is using the injured man's phone to call the man's wife in the Netherlands. Emily and I stand there for a moment. Then she walks over to his side, kneels, and takes his hand. Just holds his hand. Because it is what she can do. I see this scene now as clearly as if it had happened yesterday: The rain starting in earnest; the small group huddled together; the man, a stranger to all, in the center. And Emily, wordless, holding his hand.

To be immersed in this landscape of kindness is extraordinary. I want to stay here forever, in the drenching rain, in wet boots, in a town I don't know the name of, among strangers. In this moment, I forget about the ugliness of the world. I forget my own wounds. I am not healed. But I see, for a moment, that healing is possible.

5

"I'M SO SORRY FOR your loss."

That's what people post on your Facebook page when you announce that your animal companion of five or fifteen years has died. It is a sad event. I do not mean to trivialize it. But it is also what people will post when they discover your sister has died, or your father, or the person with whom you've spent the last thirty years, father of your children, co-adventurer, coconspirator, the one who still thought you were funny, the one who (literally) whistled while he worked, the one who got excited about compost, the one who made the best tofu in hot meat sauce, the one who bicycled with you on the shores of the Baltic even though he hated bicycling, the one who loved that chicken chop place in

Chania even more than you did, he who played the monster in many a Z-grade middle school movie shot in the woods behind the house, he who calmed the waters, he who saw the vulnerability you effectively hid from all others. And never outed you.

In the weeks and months after Tom's death, I was on the receiving end of many "I'm so sorry for your loss(es)." I knew the words were meant to comfort, and I understood the good intentions of the senders. I had uttered such words myself without realizing, as I realized then, that they might sound hollow, formulaic, generic. But I doubt there were any words that would have soothed me. I don't think we know how to express or extend solace to others. And that's because we don't talk about death until it's at our doorstep, until it knocks. And we don't want to hear the knock, and then we don't want to open the door. And when we do, we are unprepared. We are speechless.

We knew how to talk about death when it was all around us, when death was expected, when, in the late 1800s, the life expectancy was 39 years old, when 350 out of 1,000 children died before their 5th birthdays, when infectious diseases like tuberculosis, smallpox, diphtheria, whooping cough, and scarlet fever galloped through the population and claimed millions of lives. In those days, people saw a lot of dead people and went to a lot of funerals. They were fluent in the language of death, grief, and solace.

Today, in the US, life expectancy is near 80, only 7 out of 1,000 children die before their 5th birthdays, and vaccines have eradicated once-deadly diseases. We expect to live longer. We're surprised when we—our friends, siblings, partners—do not. Even when the elderly die, at ages where death is expected, we are shielded from this, because, in the US, the elderly don't often live among us. If they can afford it, they sequester themselves behind the gates of retirement communities. Or they live in fifty-five-plus trailer parks or nursing homes or memory-care facilities. Their deaths don't touch our lives in the same way they would if we lived in multigenerational households, with birth and death part of the rhythm of our days. Death itself, in our modern culture, is often seen through a medical lens, with such discussions confined to doctors and health care workers. Death is about DNR (do not resuscitate) orders or advance directives. Death is seen through the legal lens: estate planning, power of attorney. Death is their business, literally, a business, and not ours.

With a severely limited vocabulary, lacking a cultural context to support us, with little direct experience, afraid of saying the wrong thing, we say nothing or stick to homilies. But mostly, we don't engage in the conversation at all. Mostly, we avoid thinking about what to say because someone else's death reminds us that we also will die. And we do not want to think about that. There is a theory in psychology called the *terror-management theory*. It posits that when we're faced with the idea of death, this triggers "existential anxiety"—no definition needed there—and we defensively turn to things we believe will shield us from death, protect us from the emotional impact of the topic. Avoidance and denial are top of the list. Using those familiar homilies ("I'm so sorry for your loss") also works. It may be that expressions like this actually insulate us from feeling too deeply.

You would think that the pandemic would have taught us something about the language of death. But those first three years, instead, made the conversation about statistics: How many died in each state, in each month, in each age group, in each vaccination category. The numbers were big—considerably more than a million people died in the US from COVID—but numbers are their own language, and it is not the language of empathy. Numbers often do not open conversations; they close them. And close us off emotionally. This is called, in the world of psychological research, *statistical numbing.* So, as we lived through this time, we tracked the numbers. We talked about the numbers. If the conversation wasn't about infections and deaths, it was about numbers of days to stay isolated, how many feet was a safe social distance, parts per million of infectious droplets breathed in in how many cubic feet of space, how many minutes we should stand in front of a sink and wash our hands.

The language of numbers also became, and reinforced, the language of ageism. COVID killed mostly older people. Of the 1.13 million COVID deaths in the US reported by the CDC in the first 3.5 years of the pandemic, more than 80 percent were among those older than 65. Do you remember the conversation? *They would have died anyway.* Crueler still was the viral spread (pun intended) of "boomer remover." The callousness of that, the anesthetizing statistics, the confusion and anxiety of the time, the lockdowns, the Zoomification of life: Where was the space to talk about death?

I tried to dam the anticipated tide of "So sorry for your loss(es)" by not publicly "announcing" Tom's death. What was I going to do? Write an obit and pay the local newspaper to print it? Post it on Facebook? Tweet it out? Twitter was still Twitter then. I guess people do that, but I did not. Tom hated Facebook. He hated all social media. He didn't hate it out of ignorance or technophobia.

He was not a Luddite. He hated it, I think, because he considered Facebook overwhelmingly superficial, solipsistic, and self-referential, and Twitter a steaming garbage heap of nasty, ill-informed, or self-promoting content. All fair points. I thought it would be an insult to him to use social media to inform others of his death. And I knew that any public announcement through any means was just not how we, both of us individually, together as a couple, or as a family, operated. We were a family of introverts. Tom and I both gave public speeches in front of large audiences and did "media" when a book came out, but we did not socialize when we didn't have to. Our family referred to all non-family as "OPs," other people.

Many people "knew" Tom because he held, at one point, an important and visible administrative position at a university. Those folks who knew him from those days, but didn't *know* him, and probably knew me even less, would be the ones to respond through social media, the ones to click on the sad face that was meant to represent caring. I did not want to attract attention. I did not want to invite strangers into my, our family's, sorrows. Tom, in the days just before his death, had spoken and said goodbye to his three sisters. I wrote separately to each of his four close male buddies: the eccentric physicist, the shaman, his dream group buddy, and the library archivist. For what then seemed like a long time, but may have been only a few very long days, I reached out to no one. I spoke about his death to no one other than our children, who were there, in the moment, and, of necessity, to a quietly empathetic woman at the funeral home.

But the word got out. And the performative condolences poured in. I am a little ashamed to say that, at the time, I wrote a rather harsh little essay about performative condolences and the whole "I'm so sorry for your loss" thing, which I posted on my blog site. This halted many of the so-sorry comments with the exception of one from a guy I knew in high school, who wrote: "Just read your blog," which was, to repeat, about I hate "so sorry for your loss" comments. And then he added, "So sorry for your loss." I didn't find much to laugh at in those days, so I thank him for this.

Worse than the sad-face emoji and the generic expressions—and by *worse*, I mean more deeply painful to me—were the strangers who reached out to me with their memories of Tom. I wondered if I were alone in this, in not wanting to hear charming stories about how kind and brilliant my husband was. Had I been talking with a grief counselor or a therapist, which I was not, I would have asked. Had ChatGPT been available then, I would have typed in a query. Now I can do this, so I did, and this is what I learned: "Sharing memories can serve as a stark reminder that the person is no longer present, emphasizing the permanence of the loss. This realization can be overwhelming and painful for some individuals." Like me. Also, "Memories often evoke a sense of nostalgia, which amplify the longing for the person who has passed away." But perhaps those who shared were themselves grieving. I didn't think of that. I thought only of my own pain, my family's grief.

I am writing this two and a half years after his death. Yesterday, a person who knew my husband in those university days, the school's chief photographer, PMed me an image. It was a nicely staged photograph used to sell products to alumni in the university's magazine. Tom is standing in front of the wooden bleachers at the old Hayward Field, the iconic track-and-field facility at the University of Oregon, wearing a logoed raincoat, holding a pair of binoculars in his right hand. My focus went to the hand, his long, graceful fingers, how he played ragtime and Mozart and show tunes on the piano and never thought he was very good, but he was. His face. I had forgotten how young he once was, we were. And although I had not cried over him in months, I cried.

Back then, in the days and weeks following Tom's death, as the word continued to spread, true solace came from those who said nothing and offered without asking, and—surprisingly—not from people with whom I shared a long history. And—perhaps more surprisingly—not from people who knew Tom or who knew or related to me as part of a couple. I am not sure, even now, what to make of that. Maybe it was because I perceived the reactions from those who knew "us" as pity for me. And pity was absolutely not what I wanted or needed. Pity made me feel small and even more vulnerable than I already felt.

In that first tender, confusing week after his death, when I could not, and did not want to, gather with my children to cry and try to comfort and cry some more, when I did not want to open an email that began "I didn't even know he was sick," I called Karuna. We did not have one of those I've-known-her-since-grade-school kind of friendships. In fact, we had known each other for maybe four years, but the bond we felt, from the beginning, was profound. Tom had died on Friday. I called her on Monday. On Tuesday, she took off work and drove an hour and a half to spend the afternoon with me. We went for a hike. We hardly spoke. On Thursday, she drove down again. It was a warm fall day. We sat outside at a café and drank lattes. She made me laugh. I don't remember what she said. I do remember how I felt. Alive.

A while later, a FedEx truck delivered a package from Spoonful of Comfort—chicken noodle soup, rolls, and chocolate chip cookies—sent cross-continent by my literary agent. We had known each other then for barely two years. We had never met in person. An agent is a business acquaintance. Communication is generally transactional. Heather was, from the get-go, far more than that. A woman who worked in the world of words, she understood this was not the time for words.

A week or so later, another package arrived. It was from Ann, a high school acquaintance, a fellow journalism nerd from those days. We had reconnected at the one and only high school reunion I attended some years back, found that we liked who each other had become, and started a Facebook friendship. Although I hadn't posted a notice of Tom's death, I had posted a link to that essay I wrote ranting about performative condolences, and the subtext was easy to discern. Which she did. Ann didn't comment on the essay. She knew how hollow words of solace could be. She *knew*. She had lived through almost three decades of everyday, bone-deep sorrow. She had told me a story about this when we were catching up with each other.

Her first and oldest child, Jody, had been born with the severest of disabilities. I have forgotten the name of the syndrome. Ann and her husband had three more children, all healthy. She had a stellar career as a teacher. And all the while, at home, was Jody—tended, cared for, talked to, part of the life of the family—Jody who, Ann later told me, had the cognition of a four-month-old when she died at age twenty-seven. How she had lived through the darkest of times, how she kept going, I do not know. But she did so much more than endure. And she learned more about grief than anyone should ever have to learn.

In the package she sent was a little book I had never heard of but that was, I learned, a beloved and best-selling classic, *The Boy, the Mole, the Fox and the Horse.* It is one of the sweetest, most charming books I have ever read, a slender volume of ink sketches and aphorisms that could be treacly but are not. It is deceptively simple, insightful, kind, full of heart—and not about death. The evening the book arrived, I sat at the kitchen table for yet another solo dinner and read it through, front to back. Then I opened it to a random page. It was a Friday evening. Fridays, the day of Tom's death, continued to be almost atmospherically different to me from the other days of the week. I opened to a double-page spread. On the left, the boy is astride the horse. "We have such a long way to go," he is saying to the horse. On the right, the boy and the horse are looking out over a vast landscape. "Yes, but look at how far we've come," the horse says to the boy. I stopped eating and stared out the window for a long time. Did I have a long way to go? Had I already come a far distance? I didn't know the answer to either of these questions.

6

SEEING A COUNTRY LIKE this, step by (literal) step, slow, regardless of how quick my pace, alternately alone and enmeshed in random cohorts of international hikers: There is a peculiar rhythm to this that I have never before felt. Some days, I relax into it and let whatever is going to happen, happen. Other days, or parts of days, I struggle. Just when I need and want to be alone with my thoughts, here comes a loud and loquacious young Londoner who introduces himself as "Harry…like the prince, like Potter," and proceeds to lecture me on the Aristotelian theory of the ultimate nature of reality. He is twenty-two and knows everything. Except, apparently, how to read people, which they don't teach at Oxford. Or he hasn't taken that course yet. Just when he moves on to attach himself to a group of young women who may be more receptive to his charms than I am, a much older man, an Irishman, takes up the slack and begins to match his pace to mine. The Irish, it is said, are great storytellers, and Michael is part of that tradition. The story he is choosing to tell, as we walk past fields of just-harvested wheat and sunflowers, is about his bunions. The tale involves ice packs and hot soaks and splints and orthotics and, finally, surgery. He has before-and-after x-ray images of his foot on his phone. Which he most generously shares with me.

And then, just like that, I am alone again. Okay, not exactly "just like that." Michael stops for a pint at an outdoor café in a little village we are passing through, and although I would love—and need—a café con leche, I tell him I must continue on if I am to make it to my albergue in time to secure a bottom bunk. This is not exactly true, and not exactly not-true. But it does get me out of hearing the next chapter of the Saga of the Bunion.

I walk on. There is a river to cross, and yet another lovely stone bridge, and a clear path ahead: olive groves in the foreground, blue-purple mountains in the distance, a sky that threatens rain. I feel comfortable. I feel comfortable in a way I cannot remember feeling since I was a child. I am in a foreign land, among strangers, where I know just enough of the language, and not enough of the culture, finding (and sometimes not finding) my way. I am often clueless. Yet I am also at peace. It makes little sense to me. And that fact alone would throw me off-kilter, yet it doesn't. It may be that now, after all that has happened, it takes more to off-kilter me.

I listen to the *click-click-click* of my hiking poles. That is the rhythm. I pick up the pace to change it. And for a moment, I lose myself in that rhythm, in the clicks, in the sound of my own breath. This is close to a meditative state, I think, and the moment that thought pops into my mind, I am back in the world with my sore collarbone and my beginning-to-flag energy due to not stopping for that café con leche so that I could put distance between myself and Bunion Man.

Ahead, I see a trio of people, then a few more, then a gathering of at least a dozen, which qualifies as a crowd on the Camino. They have stopped in front of a stone wall. I welcome an excuse to offload my backpack. I retrieve the mostly unread guidebook I stashed in a side pocket. It tells me I have arrived at one of the great landmarks of this Camino, the famous Bodegas Irache and its wine fountain. The wall is part of what used to be a Benedictine monastery that dates back to the eighth century. In the center of the wall, at shoulder height, inset like a crèche, is what looks like a modern drinking fountain with two spigots. From these spigots, free to all who stop here, is red wine from the Irache winery. This is a gift to the pilgrims, one of those magic moments on the Camino that really do seem like magic unless you've already read about it in a guidebook or on someone's blog. Apparently, the well often runs dry, so to speak, before noon, as there is only so much wine allotted for each day. My fellow pilgrims are helping to make that happen now, filling water bottles and bota bags. When my turn comes, I cup my hand under the spigot and then drink what doesn't leak through my fingers. It is enough. It is barely 9:30 in the morning.

I arrive at today's stopping place, the small, picturesque town of Los Arcos, in the midafternoon. Like so many of the stops along the Camino, it is a village steeped in history and religious heritage.

I don't know the rich details, but I know what I see: the baroque church that dominates the skyline; the lively Plaza Mayor (town square) surrounded by centuries-old stone buildings with decorative facades and rounded arches; the cobblestone streets, so charming and so hard on the ankles. One of the benefits of setting out before dawn—and of limiting my imbibing at the Irache wine fountain—is this time I have to explore. I had made a reservation at an albergue the night before, and I have an address. All good. But my confidence is almost immediately eroded when I try to follow the little map in the guidebook. In this town, there are neither street signs nor building numbers. I am in the oldest, windiest medieval neighborhood, with narrow, serpentine lanes that keep leading back to the same spot. Which is not the site of my albergue. I have met people on the trail who are averse to a technology-enhanced Camino experience. I understand, and I respect them. There is a purity to that. But I do carry my phone. I take photographs, I record voice memos. And I latch on to any free Wi-Fi I can find. At this moment—and many others—I wish I had an operational calling plan that gave me data access.

I've arrived early enough in town so that there are not yet many pilgrims walking the streets, no one with connectivity to ask for help. I do ask a few local folks I pass, but two have never heard of my albergue, and two give me directions that I am unable to follow. That's one of the problems with knowing just enough language to ask questions but not quite enough to understand the answers.

And so I wander. Down one cobblestone street, I come upon a little shop with writing materials displayed in the window. I did not bring a journal or even a small reporters' notebook with me, in a silly attempt to save on backpack weight. I have been missing something to write on. Voice memos on my phone are helpful, but it's not the same. I need a notebook. Now I have stumbled upon a place to buy one, and even more miraculously, I remember (from eleventh-grade Spanish) the word for *notebook.*

I enter the tiny store, smile at the man behind the rough plank of a wooden counter, and ask for a *cuaderno.* He has many, which he takes down from shelves behind him and displays for me on the counter. I choose a compact, bright blue spiral one. I pay, and as I am leaving, I show him the listing for the albergue on my phone and ask if he knows where it is: *¿Sabe usted dónde es esto?* He looks at the phone, looks at me, looks at the phone again, and laughs. Then he points across the street, as in *directly* across from his shop. "*Aquí*," he says, still laughing.

I do get my bottom bunk. I do get my shower without having to wait in a line. I wash out socks and underwear in a sink with no stopper (jamming one of the socks in the drain hole) and tepid water, nothing out of the ordinary, and hang them on a line in the small courtyard, hoping to catch a sliver of sun. And then it's time to wander again, as the cafés and restaurants won't open again until six.

On the Camino, you get up every morning and follow the path to the next stopping point. There is a calming predictability to that. But so much of the daily trek, as I experience it, is surprising and unforeseen. Sometimes it's the landscape. Sometimes it's the little villages I pass through. More often, it is the people. A few days before, I had met a group of four women from Illinois who were traveling together. An odd quartet, I thought, with an age range from early fifties to almost eighty, and a personality range from Mary Poppins to Eeyore. We got to know each other in that fragmented, shorthand way you get to know people on the trail—a snippet here, a snippet there. Since that first encounter, we'd happened upon each other randomly, as our hiking paces are quite different. This early evening, after my blissfully non-backpack-burdened wanderings around the town, my feet happy in flip-flops, I find a bustling restaurant attached to an albergue. I have no idea where I am or how to get back to my own albergue, but I refuse to think about that. I think instead about the roasted-meat-scented air and boisterous laughter coming from the large dining room. It is packed—eight long wooden tables arranged in two rows—with almost no empty seats. But, this being the Camino, with its storied Camino Magic, I find one empty seat at the farthest table, where, it so happens, the Illinois quartet is seated.

I know one of them, Susan, better than the others because she has the quickest pace, and so we have found ourselves walking together for an hour or two. But it is Joan who interests me the most. On the trail, she walks slowly and encourages you to walk ahead. She will catch up at the next village, she says. And she often does. She is seventy-nine, birdlike in body, with eyes that dart everywhere and take in everything. There is so much energy—not the quick kind but rather the banked kind—in that tiny body, so much warmth that is not expressed in words but rather in the way she cocks her head when she looks at you and listens, really listens.

At dinner that night, a raucous pilgrim meal in an impossibly crowded room, she asks for a second bottle of wine, even though the five of us have yet to polish off the first one. The modest "table wine" here—unlimited quantities of which are included with the pilgrims' meals—is as good or better than a thirty-dollar bottle of wine at home. But when you know you'll be getting up before dawn and hiking all day, you limit yourself.

Joan gets up and takes the new bottle over to a table with four South Korean girls we have seen along the trail and pours them each a glass. And then takes the bottle over to the next table where three guys, Italians, sit. One gets up and hugs her. Another smiles, then says slyly but loud enough for others to hear, "You want to get us drunk and take advantage of us, don't you?" Joan pats him on the back and leaves the bottle. It seems, somehow, amid the noise and activity of the room, many have been watching Joan's perambulations. There is applause. There is hooting. Joan grins, ducks her head, and walks back to our table.

The next morning, predawn, I encounter an Israeli man whose parents fled the erstwhile Soviet Union. Like many Israelis, he has spent close to three years in mandatory military service, which means, among other things, he has regularly hiked fifty miles with a fifty-pound backpack. This is not a person to whom I mention my twenty-pound pack and my aching collarbone. He speaks six languages, drinks seven espressos a day, has actually read *War and Peace* in its entirety (if he is to be believed), knows a lot and carries the knowledge lightly, makes the day fly by (maybe an exaggeration), and, that evening, in the unplanned company of others, shows yet another area of expertise: The man can hold his liquor. These days have been so full of people. These nights have been major social events. Am I suddenly just having a good ole time and not attending to matters of the heart and soul?

I confuse myself. I want solitude and company. I want long, long silences and lively conversation. I want predictability and surprise. I want to be here. I want to be home. The following morning, alone on the trail, I stop to sit on a boulder, retrieve my new blue cuaderno, and start to write. I don't write poems. I don't think in poems. But when I look at the line spacing between my words, I realize I have written one:

Suppose you crave both adventure and domesticity,
the call of the dirt path
and the gravitational pull of the garden,
the magic of awakening in a tent
and the delight of luxuriating between soft linen?

Suppose you spark to spontaneity
but love making lists?
Suppose you love to go-go-go
but are drawn to stop and wonder?

Suppose you want to lose yourself
but also find yourself
go out into the world without a backstory
but excavate your own past?

Suppose you want to be visible and invisible?

Suppose you want to be loved but left alone?

7

IT WAS CLOSE TO ten when Lizzie left, driving Tom's car, which I told her I would transfer into her name. The boys stayed over that night, the night Tom died. They both had partners waiting at home, but they remained in the house after the hearse took Tom's body away, after we removed the sheets and blankets and pillows from the hospice bed, after we collapsed the bed and wheeled it out of the living room and onto the front porch because no one wanted to look at it, after we rearranged the living room furniture so the space looked like where we had long gathered as a family instead of where one of that family had just died.

Jackson slept upstairs in his old room, which I had transformed into a guest room but still had all his *Harry Potter* books in the bookcase. Zane slept on a couch in Tom's office. I had transformed his old bedroom into my pandemic gym. Lizzie didn't stay. I wanted her to. I wanted everyone in the house, every one of the once-there-were-five-now-there-are-four family together, even if we were in separate rooms, even if we did not talk anymore that night. But she felt compelled to leave. Maybe the weight of all that had happened in this space was too much for her. I thought, if the weight were, even for a few hours one night, resting on all our shoulders, it would be lighter for each of us. I don't think Lizzie thought that way. I think, but I am not sure, that she may have felt more of the weight than the boys, more even than I did. Tom was her hero. Tom was a safe haven. If I was the grown woman she didn't want to become (who wants to be like her mother?), he was the grown man she may have wished—or dreamed—she could someday find as a partner. And I don't mean in a creepy Freudian way. I mean she valued and admired his qualities. In that moment, that night, I did not think any of this. I was not thinking. Or feeling. It did not enter my mind that Lizzie might be leaving us to find other ways to lighten the weight, to temporarily obliterate the pain.

She would be driving three hours over to the small town on the coast where she had been living in a little getaway house Tom and I had bought during the real estate downturn. The family had spent time there during summers, and during the winter, Tom and I had used it as a writing retreat. Unlike home—the big house, the five acres—there were few chores to interrupt our days, and—because we didn't pay for it—no Wi-Fi to distract us. But Lizzie had been living in that house for the past two and a half years, working various culinary and food service jobs and, we thought, we had hoped, getting her life together.

The road over to the beach town was mostly along windy two-lane highways, challenging if you didn't know the way (which she did), somewhat frightening if you were not a confident driver (she was), and, regardless, just a long way to go after the day we had all had. It was after 1:00 a.m. when she called me. The boys and I were still sitting on the living room couch we had moved back into place. Maybe we were talking. Maybe we were staring off into space. Or hugging. Or crying. Probably all of the above. Lizzie called to say that she had made it back to the beach house. It was thoughtful of her to check in. If my brain had been functioning, I would have been worrying about her on those dark roads late at night, alone in his car, alone with her pain. I thanked her for calling. I told her I loved her. There was a long silence.

Then she told me why she had really called. Less than a mile from our house, less than a minute into her drive back to the beach, she had hit a deer. We had all hit deer on that road, every one of us. I held the record at three. Especially in the fall, the deer seemed particularly clueless or high-spirited. They leaped out from the dense bushes and forest that lined the road. You didn't see them until your headlights caught them. You braked; you swerved; you hit them anyway. The damage was almost always worse to the car than the deer, with a dented bumper or banged-up license plate, the deer leaping away into the bushes with maybe a grazed hindquarter.

But the encounter between Tom's car and the deer that night was more serious. Lizzie was not hurt, but the deer lay by the side of the road, and the car suffered a bashed-in hood, a seriously crunched bumper, and a busted headlight. Later, she sent me the pictures. But it was drivable, so she drove it. This was a deeply unnerving way to end what was probably the most intense day in Lizzie's life. In all our lives. When I listened to her recount the accident, I was beyond registering anything other than she had not been hurt, but the car was in bad shape. When I hung up the phone, I was both filled with admiration for Lizzie for handling this situation on her own and saddened that she hadn't depended on her family, just a mile away, to help. And then, the next day and the days and weeks after that, I was immersed in the chaos this caused: the phone calls and reports and documents and uploads and photographs that would be necessary, the extra confusion because the car was Tom's and the insurance was in his name, the difficulties with repair, as there were no collision shops within twenty-five miles of the beach house, the challenges with renting a car so Lizzie could get back and forth to work when she didn't have a credit card. This became part of the turmoil of the days that followed. But it was also its own special kind of turmoil, the kind Lizzie had been causing for years.

She was such an easy baby. One of my favorite pictures of her, which sums up her babyhood, is of her lying in a patch of sun on the carpet in the living room in front of the floor-to-ceiling windows that face out to the forest behind the house. She is grinning a toothless grin, her arms outstretched ninety degrees from her little body, in that completely innocent, nothing-can-possibly-hurt-me position that little babies can have. She was maybe four months old.

She was a beautiful baby, a beautiful child: honey-blond hair, slate-blue eyes, and tawny, creamy skin. She was mellow and even-tempered. She, mysteriously, gloriously, suffered not a single ear infection during her entire infancy and babyhood. No rashes. No scary spiky fevers. She was a good eater, a good sleeper. "You lucked out," my father-in-law told us every time we visited.

Lizzie heralded a new era. I was no longer the only female in the house. After those six boy-only years of purchasing anything I could find that did not feature the logo of an NFL team or a dump truck, I could now shop for adorable knit hats with crocheted roses on top, and onesies dotted with tiny purple irises, and little green velvet dresses. I could hunt for booties that looked like Mary Janes. I could send away a lock of her hair to a company in Denver that crafted "just-like-me dolls" complete with matching nightgowns for her and the doll. I saw the political incorrectness of it all, but I couldn't help myself. It was my chance to braid hair, to play with Polly Pockets.

For a while, Lizzie wouldn't wear anything but dresses. She wore this pink tutu I bought her until it was torn in so many places that it actually fell off her body. She was the princess in all the little adventures her older brothers created for themselves and for her. Tom and I had built a beyond-rustic treehouse in a big oak on the side of the property, basically a platform with railings. The ladder up to the platform was lengths of wood hammered into the trunk at step-friendly intervals. The boys would help her up the ladder, one in the lead calling encouragement, the other behind to boost or catch. She'd sit up there cross-legged and direct the boys to protect the castle, fight off the bad guys, and send up provisions. There was a long rope tied to the railing. She'd throw it down, and the boys would attach a pail filled with fruit leather or juice boxes or crackers, which she would haul up and enjoy in royal fashion. And things were good. For the first ten years.

On early-release Wednesdays, I would pick her up at school, and we would go roller-skating or bowling or hang out at pet shops or play dress-up at home. We did projects. We baked. We read our way through Beverly Cleary's eight-book *Ramona* series. We created costumes for the unsurprisingly uncooperative cat. At night, I would curl up next to her on top of the covers of the four-poster bed that had been mine as a child and rub her back until I heard her breathing deepen. Those were the years, that first decade or so, when you get a free pass. When Mommy is a saint and a genius, beneficent, perfect, the font of everything cool. This is how it was for us. Yes, there were battles—of course there were—but they were really more like low-risk skirmishes, easily settled: Yes, you can watch an extra half hour of TV; no, you can't have a cookie for breakfast.

And then, the mother ceases to be the goddess. And then the daughter needs to figure out who she is and whom she wants to be. And the relationship moves to its next phase, by turns intimate and chilly—I mean white hot and arctic cold. It is not an easy ride, nor should it be. I didn't understand that when I was a daughter pushing back against my own mother, but I did understand it when I was the mother. In fact, I researched it. I studied it. There is so very much written about this relationship, so much psychologizing, so many depictions in novels and films, so many earnest conversations on podcasts.

And then there is the real-time living of it.

Teenagerhood came early to her, as it does to a lot of kids these days. She was ten-going-on-fifteen. She had budding breasts. She got her period. She got attitude. I tried to take solace in the fact that her pushback, her back talk—but worse, her silence—her slamming the door in my face (literally and otherwise) meant she was confident in my love. My love was *not* conditional. She could be nasty to me. She could act out her teenage angst, confusion, proto-power, whatever, and she would not lose my love. When I read about this in books about parenting teens, it comforted me. And it made me realize how much I had thought, at her age, throughout my life, that I had to perform to be the beneficiary of parental love. We would weather this. We would be okay.

Something happened in middle school. I don't know what. Hormones? That complex web of insecurity and anxiety, immaturity and jealousy, that can lead to the "mean girl phenomenon," the air one breathes inside a middle school? Toxic social media? Something I should have noticed but didn't? This was not just about me now, not just about pushing back, about elbowing her way into independence. She had trouble making and keeping friends. The kids she befriended or tried to, especially the girls, had issues. Sometimes pretty big issues.

One girl, I remember, lived with her mother, who was an alcoholic and was, Lizzie recounted to me, being threatened regularly by her physically abusive ex-husband. There was a sketchy boyfriend—the mother's, not the girl's—in the mix. The friendship was, it seemed to me, a lot of Lizzie listening to tales of this girl's messed-up homelife. The girl invited Lizzie over one Saturday. I didn't want to say no, because this was a friend, and she didn't have many. But given what Lizzie had told me about the homelife, I didn't want her spending unsupervised time in that apartment. My compromise was to drive her over to the place and stay there. I chatted with the mother. I helped clean up the kitchen. I sat and read a book. I took the two girls out for ice cream. I think I was discreet. I really don't know. The friend was not a friend for very long. There were others. They came and went.

In high school, she befriended a brilliant kid, a senior, a boy who'd been abandoned by his mother, whose father made hash pipes for a living, who lived in a dilapidated apartment that, had someone from Child Protective Services gotten wind of the situation, would not have been his home. The boy and his father were often at each other's throats, sometimes, according to Lizzie, literally. One night, the boy stuffed some belongings in his school backpack, walked out the door, and started living on the street. He slept on a bench by the downtown bus station, which is where, one cold night in early spring, we picked him up in our car and drove him back to our house. He stayed with us, sleeping out in Tom's detached office. But he was, we were all aware, a friend with benefits. So sometimes he did not sleep alone. Lizzie was sixteen then. She had been to her first gynecology appointment. The boy stayed with us, talking physics with Tom, going to school every morning with Lizzie, through the final months of his senior year. He graduated with top grades. He went to an elite college on a scholarship. Lizzie did not know how to, or maybe didn't want to, save herself. And she did not allow us help. But she did, I believe, rescue that boy. I hope she realized that.

For a while, before and after that boy, it seemed she had found a niche. She loved the culinary program at her high school and was a top member of their catering team. She had an internship at a neighborhood bakery. She was on the track-and-field team, competing (and often winning) in discus. I was less worried. Then one day, we got a call from the vice principal to come into school. Lizzie had been found with a water bottle filled with vodka in her backpack. She said it wasn't hers. She said she was holding it for some "friends" and would not name the friends. At the time—and even now—I couldn't decide which was worse or which might have been more of a clue to what was going on in her life: that my daughter was drinking or that so-called friends had enlisted her to be a mule and had taken advantage of her. She was suspended for a week. It was required that she go to counseling. I remember an enormous amount of pushback about this. I remember her reports, delivered dismissively after each of the four mandated sessions, about how lame the counselor was, what a waste of time it was, how the whole thing was a joke. Her opinion about therapy and counseling never changed.

And then things quieted down again, part of the roller-coaster ride of those years. I took her on an overnight train trip to California, an adventure we both enjoyed. I took her with me to a hiking-and-health resort in Utah, an adventure that only one of us enjoyed. She hated the hiking, *really* hated it, and made sure I did not forget this. Still, we weathered that storm. Those days, we talked a lot, sometimes nonsense, sometimes serious stuff (mostly boys). The final two years of high school zipped by. She was doing well. I have photos of various culinary events at school: Lizzie, in her white chef's coat and toque holding out a platter of samosas and biryani, grinning; Lizzie behind a beautifully arranged buffet table at a catered event, looking confident. I have videos on my phone of her competing in track-and-field events: circling, twirling, whipping around the throw circle, gaining momentum, and letting fly the 2.2-pound metal disc. The strength and grace of that move. The mix of intensity and determination on her face.

But my favorite image from that time in her life, in our lives, was of her perched on the back of my older son's motorcycle, a Honda Nighthawk he had bought for himself during college. It was a warm night in early June. She was wearing a strapless, electric-blue formal gown that had taken us multiple trips and hours of scrolling to find. Her hair was up in a French twist. Her eye makeup was flawless. She had perfected these skills, self-taught, since early middle school. The two of them had set this up. She used our car to drive to within a few blocks of the venue, because her dress and her hair could not have withstood the seven-mile motorcycle trip. My son met her there on his bike. And then, slowly, with fanfare, he delivered her to her senior prom.

8

TODAY, EIGHT DAYS, NINE days into this journey—have I really lost count already?—I walk for hours up the rolling hills and down the soft valleys of the Rioja, Spain's famed wine country. The land is carpeted with vineyards, scores of furrowed rectangles that form a patchwork of green stretching to the horizon on either side of the narrow Camino path. It is just before harvest. Big fat clusters of blue-black grapes hang like ornaments from the thick vines that wrap around the trellises. Sometimes a rustic fence separates the vineyard from the path, but mostly there is no barrier. You can reach out your hand and touch the grapes. They are perfect spheres and smooth-skinned. I stop to take photographs with my phone, trying to capture whatever that color is—indigo, plum, aubergine?

The landscape is so overpoweringly lovely, both close-up and distant, the late-morning air warm but not too warm, the silence broken only by a birdcall or the click of a fellow hiker's walking sticks, that I fall into what feels like a drunken reverie, as if I've had a glass or two of this Tempranillo wine. I know what it tastes like, not the top-shelf stuff that many of these wineries produce but the pour-from-a-jug-in-the-kitchen-into-a-carafe-for-the-table variety, the unlimited pilgrim-meal wine. It goes down easy and smooth, smooth enough so that you have to be careful. My unsophisticated taste buds recognize fruity but not too sweet. There are other wine-aficionado descriptors I read about when, sitting on my bunk bed that evening, I soak up some free Wi-Fi and educate myself: dried fig, cedar, tobacco, leather, even—whatever this means—"barnyard." But mostly it's just soft, mellow table wine shared with people you just met, taking the edge off hard days.

I learn that the region I walked through all this long day and part of yesterday is home to more than 500 wineries, and that it is 245 square miles, which, if this helps visualize its vastness, is slightly larger than the boroughs of Queens, Brooklyn, and Staten Island combined. (It is also as big as 191,680 football fields, but that makes it even harder for me to grasp.) Anyway: a lot of land with a soft, pleasing, numbing sameness to it, especially when experienced at three and a half miles per hour.

My next day begins, as usual, in the dark. When dawn comes, the sky is heavy with full-bellied, gray-purple rain clouds. The rain comes. And goes. And returns. The most challenging part of this is not the rain itself—I am an Oregonian—it is the clumsy putting on and taking off of the massive poncho that covers me from head to shins and drapes over the hump of my backpack. How long do I wait, protected only by my rain jacket and Idaho Potato Museum ball cap, before I find cover, unburden myself of my backpack, rummage around inside to locate the stuff sack, unstuff the poncho, reshoulder the pack, and struggle with the poncho? (Too long.) When it stops raining, how long do I wait before I decide it is safe to de-poncho myself? (Not long enough.) It's like a halting, awkward dance you never get the hang of. Finally, by early afternoon, *out comes the sun / and dries up all the rain*. And yes, I sing this to myself. Happily, no one is within earshot. The air smells entirely different, not the earthy, musty grape smell but sweet and tangy. While I was busy wrestling with rain gear and shielding my face inside an oversize hood, the landscape changed. I am still in the Rioja but on the western edge of the province. The vineyards have given way to hayfields and potato farms. The scent is from the wild dill growing along the path.

Midafternoon, I arrive in the tiny village of Grañón—human population 250-ish, says the guidebook, although no one is in evidence; goat population, at least a dozen positioning themselves on a small stone welcome plaza, munching weeds, and looking for handouts. Tonight I will be staying at what is called a *donativo*, an albergue in the ancient spirit of the Camino, a remnant of the medieval system of religious-based resting places that hosted pilgrims of yore. These donativos are not run as commercial ventures. Free for all pilgrims, they are a "work of love" operated sometimes by locals, sometimes by veteran pilgrims who have made the Camino a way of life, and sometimes as part of the local church. They depend entirely on donations to stay open. In this little village, there is also a donativo adjoining the church, where you sleep on thin mats on the floor. I appreciate the authenticity of this, but: No. My donativo is housed in a crumbing stone building—"artistic vibe," notes the guidebook without, I soon discover, much supporting evidence—and is operated by a small elderly woman from the village.

Today is the first day I walked with only a small, hastily purchased daypack, having arranged to send my big backpack ahead. I paid one of the many local companies five euros to pick it up from last night's albergue and deliver it here to the donativo in Grañón. It would take the driver nineteen minutes to cover the distance it just took me six hours to walk. My aching collarbone needed a rest. I had learned about this send-ahead option from another pilgrim I saw a few days before who carried only a small daypack. I asked, hoping to learn something about economy, how she managed to fit everything she needed in that pack. She didn't. She was carrying only a fleece jacket, a rain poncho, a hat, water, and a few snacks. Everything else would be awaiting her when she stopped for the night.

It felt like a defeat to me to do this, as if I were not a real peregrina if I didn't carry everything on my back. As openhearted and spiritually enlightened as the Camino is, I discovered that there is a "more Camino than thou" undercurrent. At the apex of the Hierarchy of Authenticity are those who walk the entire length of the Camino, carry everything on their backs, make no advance plans for accommodations ("the Camino provides"), carry a walking stick they found along the path, and eschew all technology—all except the technology that makes Gore-Tex and Polartec possible. These modern-day peregrinos do stop short of donning the rope sandals and coarse brown woolen cloaks of medieval pilgrims.

At the nadir of the Hierarchy of Authenticity are those who hire companies to curate their entire Camino experience, which includes creating a daily walking schedule, making all reservations (in private rooms and hotels, not usually albergues), and transporting baggage. Often, the baggage being transported is actual luggage, not backpacks; thus, these peregrinos are noticeably well and cleanly dressed. They have *outfits*. I would be somewhere in between these extremes with my big pack transported for me, and my newly purchased daypack, stuffed with only the essentials and weighing in at a mere seven pounds. I had to fight not only thoughts of my potential inauthenticity but also my *So you're not strong enough, huh? You need help, huh?* self-talk. In the end, the collarbone won.

I find the donativo easily. The village is compact; the Camino runs through its center; the albergue is on the path, just across from the church and a few paces beyond the tiny town square. The heavy wooden door is open. The vestibule is small and dark. In the other albergues in which I've stayed, the delivered backpacks are stacked against the wall. There is nothing here. The proprietaria, the woman who operates the establishment, is smiling in greeting. I smile back and then inquire about my *mochila*, my backpack. She shakes her head. I think maybe my Spanish is bad, so I try again, this time with hand gestures, pointing to my small daypack and opening my arms wide to show I mean something bigger. She shakes her head again. I point to the place on the floor where the backpacks would be. Again, she shakes her head. I am at a loss. Maybe the driver has not yet arrived? Maybe my pack was never picked up this morning after I left? Maybe it is lost? *It serves me right for being a wimp*, I think. I stand in the dark vestibule, weary after a long day of walking, alternately castigating myself and freaking out. Then I pull myself together, sort of, go outside, sit on a stone bench, and attempt to call the baggage transfer company to see what happened. I do not have phone service, but there is a weak Wi-Fi signal, so I attempt a call through WhatsApp. The audio quality is terrible; my broken Spanish is not much better. I am getting some kind of response on the other end, but I don't understand. "*Habla despacio, por favor,*" I say. But no matter how *despacio*, I'm still unable to figure out what's being told to me. If I were not so tired, if I were not feeling like such a loser, if most of my brain were not busy catastrophizing, I might be able to think about what to do next.

I walk a few yards to the small courtyard next to the albergue. There are a half dozen tables set out in the late-afternoon sun. At one of them sits a guy, shirtless, his bronzed face lifted to the sun, eating chunks of watermelon. I sit at the table farthest away, and although I try not to, I start to cry. He walks over, a lean and wiry man with long, wavy dark brown hair and a slightly scruffy salt-and-pepper beard. He is barefoot. He introduces himself in English. His accent is French. He asks what is wrong. If this were not the Camino, if I were not tired and scared, if his voice were not so velvety, I would not be telling my troubles to a strange man.

He listens to the story of the missing backpack, the unsuccessful conversation with the proprietaria, and the botched phone call. He tells me that he has been staying in this tiny village for almost a week, sleeping on the floor in the church donativo, sunning himself every afternoon on this postage stamp of a plaza, while he waits for his injured knee to heal. Like I did, he started the Camino in Saint-Jean-Pied-de-Port some 160 miles to the east. He doesn't think he will be able to finish. He takes charge of my situation in the gentlest I'm-not-taking-charge way. I think the French accent helps.

He walks me over to the small bar on the other side of the plaza, where he is, after his multiday stay, well known by the bartender, who is also the owner, whose brother happens to be one of the drivers for the baggage transport company I used. He explains the situation in a combination of Spanish and French, and in short order, the bar owner calls his brother, who informs him that my backpack is in Grañón. It was delivered to the restaurant right next door to the bar because the donativo does not accept backpack deliveries. We walk ten paces to the restaurant, and there it is, *mi mochila* with the Oregon patch I hand-sewed on the flap and the iconic Camino scallop shell hanging from one of the straps. And I'm crying again. I hug Alexandre. That's the name of my Frenchman. I ask if I can buy him a glass of wine to thank him and to celebrate this wonderful turn of events.

We sit at one of the small bistro tables on the plaza in the last sliver of sun, drinking generous pours of vino tinto from the bar. Alexandre goes back over there and comes out with a guitar. He tells me he plays in little clubs on the outskirts of Paris and asks me what I'd like to hear. "Anything you would like to play," I tell him.

And so, at the end of a day that has pivoted from disaster to delight, this handsome Frenchman, sitting in a medieval courtyard that could be a movie set, shirtless and bronzed, relaxed and smiling, picks up the borrowed guitar and starts to sing.

It's Bob Dylan's "I Want You." In French.

And if my husband of three decades hadn't died just shy of a year ago, and if I didn't suspect that Alexandre had slept with a parade of charmed peregrinas during his extended stay in

Grañón, and if—and this might be the real reason—I'd been able to take a decent shower in the past few days, I might have taken him up on what was clearly being offered.

That night, I sleep in the attic of the donativo, a big, drafty, low-ceilinged room. Where the rafters meet the stucco, there are hammocks of gray spiderwebs long abandoned. The room smells of wet wool and unwashed bodies with base notes of mold and mildew. There are eight of us up here, me and seven men. Next to me, my narrow, metal cot less than two feet away, is the nurse from Colorado who had tended to the man with the broken ankle, the one who fell on the rain-slicked cobblestone street, the one Emily, the Australian, had knelt next to offering solace. That seemed like such a long time ago. It might have been a week. The other six are elderly Spaniards, small, wizened men who seem to know one another. They will take turns using the single shower in the communal bathroom. The first man emerges, damp and naked, holding a small towel in his hand. The light in the attic is dim, but not dim enough.

9

DISEASE HAS ITS OWN narrative. Sickness tells its own story. We are just characters propelled by the plot. The end of the story is as different as life and death. In fact, that *is* the difference. But the plot, the roller-coaster ride of a plot, the relentless plot, the plot that erases all other plots: That is the same.

There is the beginning, the thing that shouldn't be there but suddenly is: a spot, a lump, a pain, maybe just a feeling, a dis-ease. There is that suspended moment in time when you wait for whatever it is to go away. And it doesn't. There are the internet searches that yield confusing, contradictory, and, in the end, frightening results. Maybe you don't want to know. You wait. Finally, you make an appointment. There are tests. You wait. There are "worrisome" results. That word, *worrisome*. Don't doctors know we see right through that? Don't they know we read into the word the worst-case scenario? There are more tests. There are consults, second opinions, plans. And then there is the arc of treatment, whatever that entails, with its perils and promises; its sick-as-a-dog days; its can't-get-off-the-couch days; its wild-bursts-of-optimism days.

The treatment works. That's one ending.

The treatment doesn't work.

But something else might. The plot thickens: a new chemical cocktail, immunotherapy, a stem cell transplant, an organ transplant, a promising clinical trial. And the merry-go-round or the roller coaster—choose your ride—begins again. The setting for this story, whatever its twists and turns, this story that becomes your life, is the same: the waiting rooms; the doctors' offices; the treatment centers with their reclining chairs and IV poles and infusion pumps and monitoring devices; the radiation rooms with their gray vinyl tables and their bulky linear accelerators and their CT scanners, the lead blankets, the technicians who offer tentative smiles, not knowing if the person on the table will cry or scream or suck it up.

I know all this not only as a supporting character in the story of Tom's illness but also because years ago, now more than two decades ago, I was the main character in my own little drama. "Little" because the story ended with "the treatment worked," because I am here to tell the tale, and to tell the tale of another. While it was happening, of course, it was everything, everywhere, all at once. But that's another story. This is Tom's.

It started with a reddish patch on his chest, on the left side, just over his heart. It looked like a skin rash. He ignored it. Why wouldn't he? It didn't hurt. It didn't itch. It didn't look pretty, but that was a minor concern. When it grew, when it got lumpier and redder, he massaged it with vitamin E oil. It continued to grow. He continued to ignore it. It was now big, perhaps four inches across. Finally, he made an appointment with his GP, who took a look and thought it was seborrheic keratosis, a common, benign—oh, that glorious word—skin growth that can often appear on the chest. It might seem worrisome (that word again), but it wasn't. Said the doctor. Said the internet. He treated it with liquid nitrogen. It did not respond.

There was so much I didn't know at the time, so much Tom kept to himself. I don't know what he suspected at this point. I don't know how worried he was. He was not a worrier. We did not talk disaster scenario or really any scenario at all. We'd been down this road before. Both of us were now healthy and active and pain-free, living the life. His doctor finally suggested he go to a surgeon to get the growth removed. It was definitely a growth. That is how it was being referred to. The quick, outpatient surgery seemed "unremarkable," another word doctors like to use, which I guess is the opposite of *worrisome.* It was a big growth to remove, a big wound. It healed slowly, but it healed. He had a graceful, curved scar. Life went on.

And then, one morning in early June 2020, he left the house for what he said was a medical consult. With whom and for what purpose, he didn't say. And because he didn't say, I didn't ask. This was the privacy we allowed each other, not just at this moment but in our long marriage. It was a strategy—if that word can be used—that sometimes worked and sometimes backfired.

But now it was just who we were. Several hours passed. I figured he had stopped for lunch or to run errands. What never occurred to me until he returned, so very pale, with reddened eyes, with a look on his face I had never seen before, a look of profound sadness, was that he had been sitting in his car in the parking lot of a pathologist's office for two hours. The tissue that had been excised from his chest, the large but presumably benign growth? It was not benign. It was something called *undifferentiated pleomorphic sarcoma*.

A sarcoma is a soft-tissue cancer. The kind that appeared on Tom's chest was rare. Fewer than five thousand people in the US get this diagnosis. There are no known risk factors, no "reason" to get this cancer, no answer to "Why me?" And, because it was so rare, there was not a lot of research on effective treatments. In fact, within a few days, he probably knew as much about this cancer as the man who became his oncologist. Tom's background was in microbiology and immunology. He was a veteran science writer who knew his way around medical research.

What I knew is harder to explain. I knew, at the time, what Tom chose to tell me. He did not want me to accompany him to his now-quickly-arranged oncology appointments, and although this hurt me—of course it hurt me—this wasn't about me. There was part of him, I knew, that wanted or even needed the quiet support, the *just being there* I would have provided. But I think there was a bigger part of him that did not want me to see him in his most vulnerable of moments. Also, when you suddenly find yourself surrounded by strangers who know more about you than you wish anyone knew—all those stats, those findings, those readings, abdomen, liver, bones, lungs, heart, all that is you beneath the skin—maybe it is a comfort, a necessity, to keep a sense of privacy. Even from your partner. Especially from your partner. I may be projecting here. I *am* projecting here. This is just how I felt when I went on my own roller-coaster ride, when more than twenty years before I, as Susan Sontag once put it, became a citizen of the kingdom of the sick.

And so I knew what he told me and what I was able to glean from the unsatisfying material I found on medical websites. I did not know the specifics of what his doctor told him. I did not know exactly what the scans showed. He never showed me the reports. He summarized. His summaries offered hope. I found the reports a year after he died, when I forced myself to look at the folder marked *MED* he kept in a file drawer in his office. And then I knew what he knew: the very early indication that this was metastatic, the size of the tumor in his right lung, and later, the more than 600 percent increase in size of that tumor after six rounds of chemotherapy, the lesion in his liver. He knew, during that one year, three months, and twelve days between receiving the biopsy report and swallowing the end-of-life medications more of the plot of this story than he chose to reveal. He knew, absolutely, during the four months between the final scan and his final breath, that this was not a chronic disease that could be managed, a scary unpleasantness that could be treated and lived with. This is what his oncologist had initially told him. This is what Tom told me. This is what I believed, what I had to believe. And so it was that during much of the year that separated diagnosis from death, we did not talk about survival rates. We did not talk about dying. We pinned our hopes—or I did—on treatment.

After the surgery came chemotherapy, brutal and barbaric, but also, following the established cancer plotline, anticipatory and optimistic: the aggressive attack, the assault, the "war" that might be won. For seven roller-coaster months, it was possible to believe, to hope, to imagine a future. This poison cocktail, administered six times at three-week intervals, a treatment that sickened more than the disease itself: It is what you did, what he did, what I had done. It could kill the renegade cells that would otherwise kill you. It might, at least, stop them from growing. That's the necessary mindset. That's what kept you going.

For most of the first week after each infusion, Tom slept much and ate little. He spent his days stretched out on the couch in his office, shivering under layers of blankets, the heat blasting, an unread book lying across his chest. When you have an illness, a bad one, it doesn't just weaken you physically. It makes you feel helpless. When you live with someone who has an illness, when you're on the outside and you can't find the words to comfort, and the language-of-love food goes uneaten, you feel a different kind of helpless.

But then, by the beginning of the second week after each infusion, he felt better, and by the end of that second week and through all of the third, he was close to being himself. Himself with less energy and then, pretty quickly, with no hair. It wasn't the bald head that was disconcerting. Tom never had a great head of hair, but he did have a world-class beard. I had not seen my husband's chin, his jawline, the full curve of his lips for close to thirty years. Now he was hairless. The chemo, or more likely a steroid he was also taking, puffed out his face. He looked at himself in the bathroom mirror, struggling, I think, to recognize what he saw. He decided to call himself Mr. Moon. We made a song about it. We laughed.

Halfway through chemo, fueled by optimism—no scans would be taken until treatment was completed—we flew to

Costa Rica. It was not a "last hurrah." I don't think either of us thought of it that way. This was a treatable disease. It could not be vanquished. We knew that. He wouldn't be cured. But what I thought, what Tom maybe at this point thought—or at least what he told me—was that treatment could keep the cancer at bay, and we could have plenty of time together. Okay, so it wouldn't be great. It wouldn't be back to normal. Maybe, like my friend Nancy, who had been in treatment for a cure-resistant breast cancer for twenty years, he would have to go for every-other-monthly infusions or take pills or have regular scans. But Nancy was living with her cancer. Her cancer was being "managed." Tom's could be too.

And so I thought of Costa Rica not as a let's-do-this-before-you-die expedition but rather as a well-earned vacation, an escape from the chemo grind, a peaceful time in the sun. Still, this trip was undeniably different from other vacations we had taken over the years. We had explored much of Europe together, walking ten or fifteen miles a day through city streets, hiking over challenging terrain to see ruins, making our own meals in the little kitchens of apartments we rented. In Costa Rica, we went to a resort, the all-inclusive kind, just the sort of place we had scoffed at. But it is what we needed, what Tom needed, what was possible for him. We settled in. Tom took afternoon naps. We sunned ourselves by the pool and ate fresh fish and drank wine. We went on an all-day adventure to the Rincón de la Vieja National Park, where we rode on horses through the jungle past families of howler monkeys playing in the trees. We soaked in hot springs; took mud baths; were harnessed, helmeted, strapped, and clipped into a seven-station zip line. Suspended prone, we spread our arms and soared above the rainforest. We were, momentarily, invincible. I believed so much in our future—and either Tom did or he just wanted me to—that when he discovered that his wedding ring had slipped off in the mud bath, one of the first things we did when we got back home was go to a jeweler and pick out another ring. The jeweler thought we were an engaged couple, and we pretended that we were. I loved the ring we chose. He wore it until, toward the end, his hands began to swell, and I was afraid we'd have to cut it off his finger. I soaped up his hands, tugged off the ring, and placed it on my middle finger. It was too big, but not so big that it fell off.

We returned for three more rounds. The second half of chemo seemed ever-so-slightly less brutal. But if one were looking for hints that the treatment wasn't working—which I was not—they were there. During the magical third week of one of the infusions, we spent a few days at a high-desert resort. Tom took longer naps. He walked less. He coughed more. During what would be our final getaway, although neither of us knew that at the time, we rented a rustic cabin near the ocean. I have a photograph I took of Tom one afternoon. He is walking ahead of me, barefoot, on the beach, a beautiful and isolated stretch of coastline. It was warm that day, but he is wearing an oversize jacket that robs his upper body of form. His shoulders are hunched, and his head is slumped so far forward it is almost invisible. He looks defeated. I don't know why I captured that image. I never showed it to him. It is the next-to-last picture I took of my husband.

We drove back home. It was early fall. He knew then, after the postchemo scan, about the extraordinary growth of the largest of several lung tumors. What I knew was that his doctor had suggested he try another drug. It is hardly worth mentioning—but I am going to mention it—that because the drug was deemed "experimental," it was not covered by insurance. Of course it was experimental; with so few people diagnosed with this particular cancer, with no good data about treatment efficacy, everything was experimental. It is also probably not worth mentioning—but I am going to mention it—that this drug that could have made a difference, that could have shrunk the tumor, that could have prolonged a life worth living—cost more than $3,000. And that getting it was not easy. We got it. Or rather, I did. This was something, at least, I could do while he slept and coughed, while I continued to hope.

I am not wise enough to say anything meaningful about how one unearths or rediscovers or relearns what is at one's core, underneath all those layers, those years, how one unpeels oneself. But this is what Tom did after the Hail Mary pills did not work. He prepared to die. He didn't grasp onto last moments, wanting to experience something, whatever it might be, one last time: see the ocean, drive to the mountains, eat a piece of carrot cake. He embraced his own demise. He went not out but in.

It was solitary work.

I observed from the outside: How he sat on the back deck listening to the birds. How he stared at the big maple, its leaves now bright orange. How he fell asleep with a worn copy of the *Tao Te Ching* opened across his lap. What was happening inside, I do not know. Meanwhile, I worked my way through to-do lists that I kept as lengthy as possible to avoid thinking. I made soup. I finished a writing project for him. I bought high-thread-count sheets for that awful hospital bed he now slept in. I bought socks and slippers and massage oil and lavender-chamomile pillow spray. I kept doing because to stop doing meant I was admitting there was nothing I could do. Nothing to do. Tom was silent and still, busy surrendering in a way I did not understand but admired beyond anything I had ever admired about this man.

That evening—mid-October, it was still dusk—when he sat at the edge of the hospital bed we had set up in the living room, when he sat there in his jeans and the gray wool plaid shirt I had bought him, when he sat there and took the medication, he was a different man. He had come to a place of knowing. He was unpeeled.

Just shy of a year later, I went to Spain to walk the Camino Francés. I would not have expressed it this way at the time—I think I was too numb to think such thoughts, or maybe just too desperate to just *leave*—but I went to both lose and find myself. That sounds like a bumper sticker. But sometimes life does sound like a bumper sticker. As I walked, as the days became weeks, as the unfamiliar took on a pattern, I thought many times about the signs that were marking my way: the Camino arrows, the clamshells, the plaques. I thought also about those times I did not see a sign, that momentary panic. And the times when the only sign was the headlamp of someone walking far in front of me. And that was sign enough.

Only now, thinking back on it, do I realize this is how I navigated those last months of Tom's life. I came to see the signs, or I came to understand, finally, that what I was seeing *were* signs clearly marking the path he was on, that we were on:

When he stopped having a glass of wine at the end of
the day;
When one nap became three;

When he no longer walked out to the garden;
The first day he didn't get dressed in the morning;
When his feet no longer fit into shoes because of the edema;
When his hands began to swell and I removed his wedding ring;
When he could no longer walk upstairs to the bedroom;
When he stopped taking calls;
When he coughed with almost every breath;
When he sat outside, face tilted to the early-autumn sun, not sleeping, just being.

I didn't need to read reports of his latest scan or learn what his oncologist might have been telling him. I didn't need him to explain. The signs were there, each one ahead of us, each one marking the road. I know he saw much further down that road than I did. I know he was doing the work of someone facing death. For me, it was like driving at night in the fog. I could see only as far as my headlights. I made the whole trip that way.

10

THE DAY BEGINS WITH a walk through a series of sleepy villages, no one on the cobblestoned calles mayores except the occasional pilgrim. The few shops are not yet open. The villagers are either still in their beds or tending to their early-morning rituals behind closed doors. We who walk across the land and through the villages think, *How quaint, how picturesque*: the churches built when America was still the land of the Indigenous, the three- or four- or five-hundred-year-old stone houses with their splintery wooden shutters and their cracked terra-cotta-tiled roofs. Some of the houses are more rubble than house; others are shells of their former selves. Lining the narrow streets, the structures in many of these small villages are fighting against time and losing.

Some of these villages—especially the ones not designated as Camino stopping points in the popular guidebook—are in more fragile shape than others. The book divides this journey into thirty-four stages, each walking day ending in a village, town, or sometimes a city, that has the infrastructure to support pilgrims. This could be, in the smallest of villages, two albergues, a mercado the size of a walk-in closet, a bar, a restaurant. Some stopping places have more variety: a half dozen albergues, a hostel or two, maybe even a hotel. The cities, of course, are cities with all amenities. But the "walk-through" villages, maybe like the "fly-over" states, cannot depend on euros spent by those of us who hike through in our Vibram-soled hiking boots and our Gore-Tex jackets and our Atmospheric H30 compressible ponchos. Their way of life, tied to the land, to vineyards, to sheep and cows and goats and farming, is what sustains them. Or doesn't. In so many of these tiny villages, when I see anyone in the streets or in the square, I see old people. The young people are gone. They go to cities for education, for jobs, to see more than the few dozen people they might see during the day in their own home village, to live a twenty-first-century life. This is what I observe, walking through. What I discover later—when I have a bit of time, some surprising late-day energy, and speedy connectivity—is that depopulation is, and has long been, an issue for rural Spain.

I read that in 1900, 60 percent of the Spanish population lived in rural areas like the ones I and other pilgrims walk through. Today, rural folk account for 18 percent. I read that three-fifths of Spanish municipalities have fewer than one thousand residents. Many villages I walk through have perhaps a few hundred. The young people have left, and the old people are dying. For those few residents who remain and fall into neither category—and could help repopulate these villages—the birth rate is one of the lowest in Europe.

This is not going without notice. I delve deeper into the story of rural Spain, this country, this countryside I have so recently come to love. I am propped up on my pack on a cot in an albergue in Belorado, a prosperous village of two thousand (a Brierley stop), my iPhone on my knees; I learn about an initiative called Holapueblo, which has been helping people start small businesses in low-population, rural villages. The plan was created by this odd triumvirate: a for-profit company that defines itself as "a global operator of strategic electricity and telecommunications infrastructure and a key player in the green and the digital transformation for a sustainable future," a social service agency that has been helping reinvigorate rural areas since 1997—and IKEA. Villages apply for help. I read the list. It includes villages in every region I've walked through and every region I will walk through. It is hard for me not to think about Spain struggling to keep these places alive while we pilgrims walk through admiring the ruins and romanticizing the simple, rural life.

I think also about the churches. The smallest of villages has one, and even the most modest of these churches, the ones where the nave is the size of a small bedroom, where there are maybe three pews, these are exceedingly well tended: the stone floors swept clean; no dust, no cobwebs anywhere; always a small arrangement of votive candles, some lit, some waiting to be lit, set out in a tiny alcove facing a crucifix or a painting or a statue. I light a candle for Tom sometimes. I more often light one for Lizzie. She needs it more. Frequently, right inside the church, there is an old woman, a very old woman, sitting on a small wooden chair by a little table. On the table is an ink pad and a stamp, the sello we pilgrims collect in our foldout credencial to show our progress along the way. Next to the stamp is a donation jar. She is not selling the stamp. This is not the way of the Camino. But she is overseeing the action, carefully monitoring who stamps and who reaches into their pocket or fanny pack to find a coin. Out here, a euro and change buys a café con leche or a generous pour of house wine. A euro has real value. I imagine the value it might have to the elderly parishioners of a tiny church in a depopulated village. Of course I reach into my waist pack for a coin. Of course everyone does. On the far side of the village, a few feet off the path, is a vending machine positioned under a wooden lean-to. For one euro, you can buy a small bottle of prosecco. I reach into my pack for another coin.

The hike the next day is a long slog through small forests along a flat, dusty path with no views and near-ninety-degree heat. I walk for an hour or so with two jaunty women from the UK. We sing "Mad Dogs and Englishmen" while we swat flies. I love being in the presence of those who find humor in discomfort. I think the British may have a patent on this. Still, it is a relief when the path gains a bit of elevation and then dips down to offer a view of a shallow valley and the small, red-roofed village where I will spend the night.

The village, population sixty, has existed since the eleventh century and probably owes its continued existence to its designation as the end of one of the stages in the Brierley book. It fulfills all expectations of quaintness: the row houses with their stone-and-plaster fronts, the nine-hundred-year-old church with its triple bell tower, the perfectly preserved stone bridge that arches over a quiet stretch of river. I luck into a bed in a room with only three others. I go to sleep thinking about tomorrow's hike, a mere 22.4 kilometers (14 miles), much shorter than many of the previous days. And I will be walking to Burgos to meet up with my Camino pal Kiki and to enjoy my first rest day after twelve days of walking. Easy peasy, as Lizzie used to say.

Or not.

The hike begins with a challenging hill, long and rocky with flinty stones that make finding footing an obstacle course and using poles, which get stuck between the rocks, a danger. At home, I rarely think of falling and injuring myself. I've never broken a bone or torn a tendon. Scrapes, gashes, bruises? Many, but never anything more serious. This has made me a little cocky. But not this morning. This morning is all about caution; it is full of what-ifs. This is not a good place to dwell, so I think instead about how hungry I am after nearly four hours of walking powered by a single café con leche.

My habit, the habit of many pilgrims, is to stop in a village midmorning for a late breakfast of the traditional Spanish tortilla. This is not "our" tortilla. It is this country's celebrated national dish, an omelet both dense and tender, rich with olive oil, layered with velvety potatoes. The pie-shaped slices are thick and generous and inhalable. And come with a hunk of bread. As I sit at a little table outside the café and eat, it occurs to me that I have not once, in my week and a half of stopping for this breakfast, thought about or tried to calculate the calories. And it occurs to me, with both sadness and a sense of liberation, that this may be the first time since puberty that I have not thumbed through a pocket-size calorie-counter book (my companion through my teen years) or, later, googled "how many calories in . . ." whenever I considered eating anything other than a salad. Not just that; I have not once asked myself, *How many miles of hiking will it take to burn these calories?* I know there are much bigger aha moments on this journey, legitimate spiritual awakenings, the insights that have led to marriage, divorce, career change, expatriation. This food freedom is not of that elevated nature. And it may be just a temporary silencing of the body-perfection voices I have been listening to since I first opened the pages of *Seventeen* magazine. But now, this warm and bright Spanish morning, I savor my massive slice of egg-and-potato pie in a bubble of uncomplicated joy.

The day gets hotter and hotter, and the miles are not speeding by. My back, under the pack, is as wet as if I have been swimming. My socks, the silk toe socks under the woolen hiking socks, are soaked through. I am alone for an hour or so, really alone, seeing no one on the path, even far ahead of me. I could use a few jaunty Britishers or perhaps that quartet of spirited young Korean girls who are GoPro-ing their way along the Way. I read later, at home, about how crowded the Francés has gotten. So write veterans who walked the path a decade or more ago before Martin Sheen's *The Way* introduced so many to this journey. But the only times I have encountered "crowds" (as in more than a half dozen hikers) have been at albergues and cafés.

Finally, in the oven-baked heat of midafternoon, as I believe I am nearing my destination for the day, the city of Burgos, the walk turns ugly. The quiet beauty of the Castile-León landscape changes into a walk along a gritty, industrial highway that, I soon discover, skirts the airport. Both sides of the four-lane highway that parallel this stretch of the Camino are lined with car-repair shops, gas stations, warehouses, and small factories. No worse than you'd see in the US. In fact, no worse than the drive from the airport to town in my small city. But the shock of it, the shift from a green, growing world to a gray, paved one; the noise, so much noise, so loud—I have become accustomed to hearing only my own breath, the click of my poles. And the smell, the stench of diesel, the hot, musty urban air, that acrid smell of manufacturing.

I am wearing my pack again, and it feels as if someone put a few bricks in there when I wasn't looking. I feel alternately grouchy and self-pitying with a dash of anger thrown in. I heard this was a bad walk from other pilgrims. I heard there was an alternative route that went by a river. I missed the sign for the turnoff. I also heard that some people jump on a bus for a quick ride into the city. But I don't know anything about the transportation system, and without connectivity, I can't find out. I am therefore angry not just for failing to see the alternative route but also for not getting a Spanish SIM card after I discovered that my phone company's "international" plan mysteriously stopped at the border between France and Spain on that first day. I am also angry because, dammit, I am supposed to be *going with the flow.* I am supposed to embrace the mindset of "the Camino provides." But in this case, the Camino is providing an onerous walk, and the flow I am going with is the flow of 18-wheelers down a highway. And I, the pilgrim, the supremely privileged woman who gets to do this, to have this grand and perhaps healing adventure, am reduced to a cranky whiner.

The concrete sidewalk is hot. It feels as if I have been walking forever. I left the town of Agés before dawn this morning, and it is now midafternoon. I expected to be in Burgos by now.

I believe I am very close until I walk by a sign that indicates the city is still 6K away. That's close to another four miles. By car down this speedy highway, that's maybe five minutes. For me, even walking briskly—and I am all out of briskness right now—that's at least another hour and change. And then, because "the Camino provides," even if you are a grumpy, sweaty whiner, I am suddenly joined on this hot sidewalk by a small, stringy, smiling man. If you searched Google images for "spry," a picture of this guy would show up. He is a Quebecois, an octogenarian, and a pilgrim who walks without phone or map or guidebook. His wife, back on a small farm outside of Montreal, thinks he's *fou*, but they've been married for more than sixty years, so accommodations for his foolishness have been made.

All this I discover slowly, as he speaks only French—and not the kind I learned in high school back when Charles de Gaulle was president. I am digging deep. I've spent much of the past week and a half scouring my brain for Spanish, which I also learned in high school, but I get to practice at home on almost daily trips to my local grocery store, where I attempt conversation with my favorite produce guy, Rafael, born in Mexico. The French is there, somewhere. Excavating it clears my head of complaints and self-pity. And this man, this energetic, beaming, lively man who is not troubled by the heat or the highway or the fact that he has no idea where he will stay tonight, is a blessing.

We continue into town. He is maybe three inches shorter and twenty pounds lighter than I am, but he walks faster. The kilometers pass far more quickly than when I was muttering to myself. After a while, maybe it's a half hour, the highway turns into a city street, still busy, but lined with shops and cafés, with flowerpots and benches dotting the sidewalk. We stop to sit at one for a moment. I want to check my reservation. I have treated myself to a hotel for the night. I have an address but no idea about location. I tell him this, and he pats me on the back, shrugs, and offers his hundred-watt smile. His teeth are pretty good for an eighty-three-year-old's. Just then, a man walks toward us—a city resident, not a pilgrim. He stops in front of our bench, looks at us both, reaches into his pocket, and hands us each a piece of candy.

It feels—and was—anticlimactic to mention that I eventually found my hotel, that the room was big and bright, that the bed was three times the size of any bunk I'd been sleeping in, that the bathroom had a tub and fluffy towels, that I later walked into a one-chair salon and had a lovely woman shampoo my hair, and that I sat at a little table drinking a glass of vino tinto in the fading light.

11

WHAT I REMEMBER ABOUT Lizzie, what I choose to remember, is her sweetness, because to remember her after the drugs took hold, to remember her after she lost job after job, after she stopped taking care of the house, after she stopped taking care of herself, after she lived in the back of a van and ate gas station burritos, is to go down the rabbit hole of grief, to go where every parent of every child addicted to drugs goes. And so, I think instead of how she was, of her extraordinary generosity toward others, if not herself. I think of the favors she did. I reframe my judgment of those sketchy friends—some of them, not all of them—not as bad choices but as kids she wanted to save from their circumstances. I recently came across this quote: "Don't set yourself on fire to keep someone else warm." I think now that this is what she did. The fires were small at first, then bigger, finally all-consuming.

One night at dinner—Lizzie was just starting middle school then, the boys almost finished with high school—we were sitting around the table, eating and joking, when Lizzie commented, almost as an aside, that our family was not "normal." My immediate thought was that she was referring to our shared sense of humor that sometimes went beyond quirky, or that we still did the same toddler-era Easter egg hunts in the front meadow every spring with the prized "bad egg" filled with black jelly beans, or maybe that we grew some of our own food. But what she meant, she explained, was that she was growing up in a two-parent household that could afford not just the necessities but some luxuries as well, that she lived in a household where, day to day, there was little drama, few crises, two big brothers who indulged her, home-cooked dinners almost every night. It wasn't *Leave It to Beaver* (the reference would be lost on her and her brothers, of course), but there was a stability and predictability to her life that she did not see or sense in the lives of others. And especially in the lives of the kids she befriended.

Lizzie felt her privilege more acutely than most kids did, which, in retrospect, I admire and respect. But back then, I wished that she would have just delighted in what she had. Instead, it made her feel uncomfortable, maybe even ashamed. This choosing of friends from marginal circumstances was, I think now, both an expression of her true generosity of spirit and her need—perhaps because of self-esteem issues so hidden none of us saw them, maybe not even Lizzie herself—to hang out with kids who were needy, careworn, and embattled. It made her feel better about herself. What did it mean for a twelve-year-old to toggle between physical comfort and psychological discomfort, between being needy and being needed? I was busy navigating the stormy seas of the mother of an about-to-be-teen daughter. It was confusing and painful and tumultuous and overwhelming. So, of course, I decided to write about it.

I knew the road I was traveling, that Lizzie and I were traveling together, the wild ride that was the mother–teen daughter journey, was both well-trodden and mysterious. I had been a teen girl once. I remembered thinking my mother was gaspingly clueless, that every question she asked was an invasion of privacy, that she had no idea what I thought, and that I never, ever wanted to be anything like her. I was intensely—but quietly—defiant. When you're on the other side of this, the receiving end, the journey feels unrecognizably different. Lizzie may have been kind and openhearted with these kids I considered ne'er-do-wells, but she was not so kind toward me. There were snarky responses. There was door slamming. There was the ultimate weapon of all: silence. I cried. In secret. A lot.

Some believe this rocky relationship is just a phase, that if you can shut up and grit your teeth, it will be over in a few years. "That's how it used to be with me and my daughter," my friend Kay told me at the time. Her daughter was then college-aged. "Now we're really close," she said. I wanted to be consoled, but I wasn't. The truth was, the rift that opened up between my mother and me when I was twelve or thirteen defined our relationship for the next thirty years. For us, it wasn't a phase. It was the beginning of the rest of our lives. I did not want that, I could not bear that, for my daughter and me.

I did what I knew how to do: I delved into the subject like a research project. I read all the studies I could find in the annals of developmental psychology, child psychology, child development, family relations, neurobiology, sociology. I read fiction that centered on mothers and daughters. I interviewed therapists and mothers. And finally, I did what others might have thought (at the time, and now) as wrongheaded, invasive, desperate: For eighteen months, I was Margaret Mead in middle school. I sat in the back of classes, hers and others; I hung out in the lunchroom; I sat in the bleachers during gym classes; I went on field trips. I watched and listened. I tried to understand twenty-first-century teen-girl culture. And my own daughter.

Lizzie let you do this? friends asked in disbelief. Yes. And not just with grudging permission—but with curiosity and involvement. During the immersion and the writing and then the promotion of the book that emerged from the research, our relationship changed in the most extraordinary way. And for the better. She knew the world of middle school, and I did not. She knew the world of the twenty-first-century teen, and I did not. She became my guide, my interpreter. She was, all of a sudden and for her early teen years, in a position of dominance. To know more than your mother, to have your mother listen carefully to you as you explained, to hold the power of knowledge. She loved it.

I knew this at the time, and I relive it now as I look at the videos we made together, filmed and edited by my older son, that caught the dynamics of our relationship. We were so easy with each other. I had scripted the videos—snippets of mother-daughter talks where we riffed on what we agreed and disagreed about—but we went off script immediately. We had fun. We stepped on each other's lines. We exchanged looks of loving exasperation. I view these videos now—they are on and will forever remain on YouTube—and I see this lovely about-to-be-a-woman girl with her hennaed hair and her clear eyes and unblemished skin, all that promise. And it simultaneously warms and breaks my heart.

I think also of another moment from that time. I was doing some touring when the book came out and I had been asked to talk at a community arts center in a coastal town. It was a free trip to the beach, a free night at a nice hotel, and, I thought, a good little mother-daughter overnight jaunt. In one of the chapters in the book, I recounted a funny conversation between Lizzie and me, one of those interchanges that says more than it says. I asked if she would like to "perform" it with me at the event. I would be doing the author thing of reading excerpts from a podium. When it came time for that piece of dialogue, I would say my line and, from the back of the room, Lizzie—whom I would not have introduced—would respond with her line. We practiced in the car driving over. When we arrived at the venue, Lizzie, like all the other members of the audience, sat on folding chairs facing forward as I did my thing. Then I said my line. And from the back of the room came Lizzie's voice. Heads turned. She was sitting, not standing, but she was beaming, so it was hard to miss her. After the reading, she was thronged. She held court. When it was time for me to sign books, just about everyone wanted Lizzie's signature as well. I was so proud of her, of us, of what we had weathered. I thought I was, we were, home free.

And then there was high school and the sting of mean girls and the sweetness of the boy she saved and the prom no one asked her to but that she went to anyway in a gorgeous dress that made her eyes look like moonstones. But when one door closed, another one did not open. Or, at least, the door that my husband and I wanted to be opened, the one that had opened without as much as a push for our two sons—college—did not open. Because she had loved her food and cooking classes in high school, because she had briefly apprenticed at a wood-fired bakery during middle school, because as a child she had progressed from Easy-Bake Oven to Betty Crocker cake mixes to from-scratch recipes in a matter of weeks, it seemed that culinary work would be her future, at least in the short term. I knew it was hard work, ill paid, a tough road, but maybe she'd want to go to some fancy culinary institute, and maybe she'd be hired by some amazing bakery, and maybe she'd start her own company. Yes, the dreams we have for our children that they don't have for themselves. Yes, I wanted a paved road to the upper middle class for her.

What happened instead was that, with some pushing (me), she applied for the culinary program at our local community college. Maybe the pushing was more than "some." She got in. We bought the special knife set, and the white kitchen coat, and the extraordinarily expensive textbook. In her first class, the teacher-chef had them cracking eggs. Lizzie came home that afternoon all huffy because he had made her crack eighteen eggs until she got it "right." This was not a good start. The program, which led to a one-year certificate, included requirements in English composition, math, and human relations. This was met with even more attitude than the egg-cracking. There were brief flashes of enthusiasm and long bouts of crankiness layered with boredom. She was living at home, in her childhood room. But she had a car, and she soon had a part-time job at a bakery, and soon that job became more important than school. In fact, the job—her shift began after the retail bakery closed and lasted almost to dawn—made school next to impossible. And that was fine with her. She was making minimum wage, working on her feet for eight to nine hours, then coming home to sleep most of the day.

She worked four days a week. On her days off, it was impossible to shift to a more "normal" schedule, so she became a night owl who hung out with other night owls, usually at a dive bar downtown. Often ass-to-elbow crowded, with blaring metal music, the place stayed open until 2:30 a.m. For "regulars" like Lizzie, the hours were extended another hour, through staff cleanup and closing, followed by hanging out at someone's apartment. She'd return home after dawn, fall asleep in her clothes on top of her bed, wake up in time to make her shift or, if it was not a workday, go back to the bar.

We worried about this a lot, Tom and I. We talked about it. I remember that our late-night discussions focused on health. She wasn't getting good sleep. She was, obviously, drinking, and we didn't know how much. I remember that, in those days, I was particularly worried about her smoking cigarettes. How clueless I was. On the other hand, we liked that she had a social life, that she had friends. High school had been a lonely time. I liked that she was brave enough to go out on her own, to find a place she felt comfortable and accepted. I wanted to think of the dive bar as a darker, shadier Cheers where everyone knew her name. We wanted her to make her own decisions, to move into adulthood, to let her hold her own reins. "She has good instincts," Tom would say. "She'll come around." I loved that he thought that.

But her instincts were also to gather people around her who were living marginal lives, which is easy if you hang out at dive bars and frequent the apartments of people who stay up all night. Occasionally, she would not come home at all, having fallen asleep on someone's couch. She was being responsible, she told us when she showed up at the house midmorning. She was too tired to safely drive home. I believed her. I wanted to believe her. She may even have been telling the truth, at least sometimes. She was moody. But she had always been moody. And she was working a tough job, sleeping poorly, and rarely eating the healthy home-cooked meals I made, so her moodiness seemed normal and explainable. In retrospect—I so hate that phrase—we were missing something.

From time to time, she would ask if a new friend could come for dinner, and we would joyfully say yes. Yes, she would have a healthy meal that night! And yes, we wanted to know who these friends were! When your children are little, you know all their friends. You know the parents of these friends. And then, year by year, you know fewer and fewer until your no-longer-child is operating in a different universe. Once she brought home a guy who lived in the basement of a friend's parents' house with three other guys, none of whom worked, all of whom played MMOs—massively multiplayer online video games—all night. Another time, she brought home a busboy with a serious drinking problem whose superreligious parents had disowned him. She drove him back and forth to work for a while, as he had lost his license after his third DUI. She brought home a young woman who worked at another bakery in town and got Lizzie a job there for a bit more money than she was making. I liked her a lot, not just for that reason but because the girl appeared to be unburdened by some of the burdens of the other kids in Lizzie's life.

She talked about another woman, ten years older, with two kids from two different fathers. The woman came to dinner a few times, an extravagantly pierced and vibrantly tattooed person who talked nonstop. I could see the attraction. The woman was a living artwork, and one never had to worry about awkward silences, because there were no silences. Lizzie loved her kids. She baked cookies for them, made an elaborate cake for the seven-year-old's birthday, brought them little presents every time she visited, babysat when the mom went off to NA meetings, or support groups, or maybe therapy sessions. She had a lot to process, this woman, alcohol and drug addiction being number one, poor partner choices coming in a close second, Daddy issues in there too. Lizzie spent hours and hours listening to the stories of this woman's life. One ongoing story was about the father of her first child, a man named FA, who had his own deeply checkered past. It was this woman who introduced Lizzie to FA.

12

THIS CITY WAS FOUNDED in 884 by the second Count of Castille. That's a thought to sit with for a moment. At that time, on my home continent, the Pueblo people were just starting to build multistory adobe apartments, and from the Atlantic to the Great Plains, the many tribes of the Mississippian culture were busy creating settlements with a network of villages linked by trading routes. I know this because for several hours on this rest day in the extraordinary city of Burgos, I sit in one of the many coffee shops that line a broad pedestrian walk along the river, and I people-watch, and I write in my notebook, and I binge-google on my phone. This city, with its gardens and parks, its tree-lined promenades, this city rich in cathedrals and churches, convents and monasteries, castles, statuary—so very many men on horses—has transformed me, in less than twenty-four hours, from pilgrim to tourist.

Sitting in the coffeehouse, nursing my third café con leche, taking a break from walking and wandering city streets, I am shocked by how easily and seamlessly I have left the Camino behind. The Camino itself, the path, is right here in front of me. I see it out the window. It is the feeling I have left behind, the emptiness of thought that over the hours becomes a meditation, the unexpected jolts of pride that I am really doing this, the glorious freedom from things. And now, boom, I am just a visitor to a city, a sightseer. And suddenly, I want everything. I want a new T-shirt that I don't need. I want a hat (I already have two). I want that Swiss Champ XXL knife with seventy-three functions I see in the window of a shop I pass. (I have a little knife that serves me well. This one in the window weighs a whopping thirteen ounces.) I want a fancy dinner.

This wanting is such a big part of me, such a big part of being an entitled American, such an ingrained part of my identity as a (quite literally) card-carrying consumer. Why did I think that two weeks on the Camino would cure me of that? From time to time, as I've walked, I've thought about my walk-in closet at home, and how when I get back, I will scour it of unneeded items. How many sweaters does one person need? How (and why) did I ever acquire thirty pairs of socks? I've thought about my kitchen cabinets, my pantry, the shelves in my garage. So much stuff. Sure, like everyone else, I read Marie Kondo. And like most everyone else, I did nothing. I think you can't just read about this, or see videos, or be reasoned into simplifying. You have to feel it. One of the big lessons of the Camino, if I can actually learn it, is how little stuff I need. We need. I hear, from pilgrims I pass on the way, that they keep coming back to walk. Maybe they do this to try to recapture that freedom from want. And then there is the whole "creature comforts" thing. In one night, *one single night* in that hotel room with the big bed and the soft duvet, I have so thoroughly sunk back into comfort that I forget that I ever slept in a narrow iron bunk bed on a paper sheet. Some nights, I wanted to forget that. And now I miss it?

It's time to go.

Burgos sits on the eastern edge of the Meseta, the great inland plateau of the Iberian Peninsula. It is a vast, high (elevation average of more than two thousand feet) tabletop of land roughly the size of Kansas. The Camino cuts through the northern section of it, with a walking distance of an intimated 136 miles. I had heard from veteran pilgrims in albergues and coffee shops that this was their least favorite stretch of the journey, that it was long, monotonous, bleak, hot, windy—none of the adjectives were good—and that perhaps it was best, especially for first-timers like me, to skip it entirely. I learned that there was a bus from Burgos to León that zipped across the Meseta in a mere two hours for about twenty-five dollars. But I do not consider this for even a moment. It feels like cheating. And after my rest day in Burgos, alternately wondrous and filled with self-doubts about what Camino "lessons" I might take home with me, I needed some hard hiking. I needed discomfort. After the city, I wanted to disappear into this vast landscape. Also, I had connected with Kiki in Burgos, and we made a plan to walk together. We would traverse the most challengingly monotonous section, which the guidebook divided into three stages, in just two stages, two long days, the first being thirty-two kilometers, the second, thirty-seven kilometers. That's twenty and twenty-three miles, back-to-back (eighty-six thousand steps on the pedometer). My usual distances have been more in the fifteen-to-sixteen-mile range. But having a partner makes this seem not just possible but also a challenging adventure.

Hiking with Kiki—we've been on the path together a few times already—is a combination of silence, deep conversation, knowledge dumps, literary banter, random nonsense, and dark humor. That she craves and appreciates silence as much as I do makes our walking together possible. That she is both accomplished and self-deprecating makes us soul sisters and unites us across our differences, which include, for starters, that she lives in Texas (could not be more different from Oregon), that her husband is alive and well, and that she has researched the hell out of this journey, treating it like coursework for a graduate seminar. I discovered as we walked—as she talked and seemed to know everything—that she had spent two years of intense study to prepare for this trek, including joining online Camino groups, a deep reading of the popular guidebook we both disdained, months of note-taking frenzy from another guidebook I'd never heard of, a scene-by-scene analysis of that iconic Martin Sheen Camino movie I had never seen, a rereading of Book V of *Codex Calixtinus*, which, needless to say, I'd never heard of. In her backpack, she carried a black leather-bound Moleskine notebook with pages and pages of densely scribbled notes, not only about the history and religious significance of various villages, churches, monasteries, statues, monuments, shrines, and saints but also extensive notes about local oddities and food. Her notes for the day I was in Grañón being serenaded by my Frenchman read like this:

> Lunch in Azofra at Bar Sevilla? This is Chicken Town!!! (Chickens saved German boy—in CC [*Codex Calixtinus*]) eat @ la Gallina Que Cantó (calle Mayor 32). Stay at Parador! Go see chickens in Catedral de S. Domingo de la Calzada—supposedly only church anywhere that is allowed to keep animals in it?!?

If I tell you nothing else about Kiki, this is enough to know her.

To prepare for the next two days, our trek across the Meseta, where there will be long stretches between small villages, we have provisioned ourselves with snacks. One of these snacks—assorted nuts that we've divided and placed in plastic bags tucked into handy side pockets on our backpacks—is a constant source of humor. One or another of us, now I can't remember who, dubbed them "nut sacks." That we will find this consistently hysterical says much about the monotony and hard trekking of those two days.

The land, flat and featureless, stretches to the horizon. The poor soil here means little agriculture. After the fertile farmlands and dense forests, the olive orchards and vineyards of the previous two weeks, this feels like I am suddenly color-blind or have developed cataracts. Everything is a shade of brown. For a while, Kiki and I entertain ourselves by naming the tones and tints—dirt brown, desert sand, khaki, fawn, buff. Naming helps us see the land that feels unwelcoming and lonely. We're walking a dirt road that extends to the horizon. For miles, we see no others on the path. Occasionally, in the very far distance, one or the other of us notices something. What? A tree? The steeple of a church? A transmission tower? Civilization? After an hour of walking, we see that it is a lone tree. Kiki insists on telling me how many kilometers we have walked and how many we have yet to walk. I tell her, sharply, that she should keep that information to herself. So she changes the subject and starts telling me about Black Madonnas. These are depictions—paintings or statues housed in churches and shrines—of the Virgin Mary with dark or black skin. Kiki has read that these Black Madonnas have roots in pre-Christian goddess worship, representing fertility, the earth, and the cycles of nature. The dark skin might symbolize the fertile soil or a connection to the earth. When she talks, it is almost always interesting. But sometimes not as interesting as the silence. And so, we go back to that.

It takes a while to find joy in the starkness and solitude, to quiet my judgmental mind, to stop thinking of this landscape as ugly and forlorn. While I am still in the this-is-ugly mindset, I think, not for the first time, about how Tom would hate this, not just this dry, flat, brown land but the Camino adventure itself. He loved to travel—we traveled together to many places over the years—but this is not his kind of travel. And I think, not for the first time, how glad I am that I chose this thing to do that holds no memories of Tom and me, that I can experience all this without saying to myself, *I remember when Tom and I stopped here*, or *If only Tom were here*, because, even if he were still alive, he would not be here.

With the quiet between Kiki and me, I settle into the otherworldly nothingness of the landscape. I feel insignificant, which is disconcerting and at first a little horrifying—like those aha moments during the kind of "trips" I took in my twenties—but it is also freeing. There is almost nothing here. What do I need? *What do we need?* Maybe just the earth and the sky. Because right now, that is all there is, and it is enough. This Meseta is a lesson in perseverance and the blessings of small things—a breath of wind, a thin streak of cloud. It is also a lesson in simplicity that mirrors that other lesson I forgot so easily in Burgos: that I had everything I needed on my back. As one of my woo-woo friends back home would say, "The universe is trying to tell you something." More directly, the universe is telling me right now to get out of the sun. But there is no place to go. Kiki and I stop to slather ourselves with sunblock. It is almost the middle of October. The notorious unforgiving, oven-baked heat of the Meseta is not an issue. But it is plenty warm, in the mid-eighties. The sky is cloudless, and there is no shade. The afternoon, like the path, spreads out to the horizon. We have been walking for more than seven hours. Kiki tells me how much farther we have to go, and I have to stop myself from throwing my nut sack at her.

We are staying in different albergues tonight. Hers is located in a small village; mine is a kilometer or two before the village, out in the middle of the nothingness. Toward the late afternoon, I see a slight rise in the distance, a smudge on the horizon, a mirage. This must be the place. It takes an hour of hot, dusty walking to get to the uphill path leading to my resting place tonight, a simple, squarish building standing alone on a bare hillock. It is called the Oasis, and although it is not a "green spot in the desert"—there is no green to be found anywhere—I know it will serve its purpose: a refuge, a relief. Kiki continues on. We will meet up again in the morning.

This albergue is startlingly new, just built, a contrast to the centuries-old donativo back in Grañón. It seems almost deserted. I have a moment of panic thinking that it hasn't yet opened for business. But as I trudge up the path from the Camino to the covered sitting area in front, I can see a solitary figure lounging in one of the chairs. I am just greeting him when another man comes out the door. I know this guy! As so often happens on the Camino, it is someone I crossed paths with days and days ago. We stayed at the same albergue one night, our bunk beds not far apart. It is Hans, a big bear of a man from Norway who showed me pictures of his family on his phone, which were infinitely more pleasant to look at than those bunion x-rays from my Irish friend. The other man, rolling a cigarette as he drags on one between his lips, four empty bottles of Estrella Galicia on the small table in front of him, is a weathered Brit. He has the look of a hard-living aging rock star. Think Keith Richards. Not your typical pilgrim, if there is a typical pilgrim.

The proprietor comes to the door and ushers me in. "*Bienvenida*," he says, welcoming me. "*¿Cómo estás?*" He doesn't wait for an answer. He sees what shape I'm in. He takes me gently by the shoulders and leads me to a big, bright, sparkling clean room with four sets of bunk beds, one in each corner. The Brit has staked out a bottom bunk in one; Hans is set up in another corner. I get a bottom bunk in the third corner. A huge expanse of room separates us. Like the open spaces of the Meseta, there is vastness here, an emptiness I am not accustomed to in albergues. I off-load my backpack, and Federico, the proprietor, asks if I need to do laundry. He is speaking in English now. On the Camino, this is a rhetorical question. I laugh. He hands me a cloth bag and tells me to place my dirty clothes in it. He will do my laundry. This includes, as I find out an hour later, hanging my clothes on a line outside to dry. I am overcome by his kindness.

This man speaks seven languages. I ask him how many after I hear him speaking Portuguese to the cook, French on the phone, Norwegian to my trail friend. His English is fluent. He is too humble to say this about himself. When I quiz him, he admits that he has traveled the world and has lived and worked on three continents. I don't ask what brought him to this outpost on the Meseta. I think there must be a story there. If he wanted to share, he would.

Because the Oasis is not in a village or near anything at all, the place has a full kitchen that serves dinner. Hans and I make "reservations," which is funny because the two of us plus the chain-smoking Brit are the only ones here. I am expecting the usual albergue fare, the "pilgrims' meal" I have eaten almost every night: a simple salad, a piece of chicken, bread, and a small dessert. Instead, Federico brings me a plate with a generous piece of perfectly grilled salmon, a big serving of sauteed fresh vegetables, and an entire bottle of wine. Hans, who is six foot five and built like a linebacker, is—surprisingly—a vegetarian. The cook has made him his own meal. While we eat, Hans shows me pictures of his eight-year-old daughter. I tell him I have a daughter too. I use the present tense. I *have* a daughter. This walking without a backstory is liberating. For just this moment, I want to pretend Lizzie is still here, waiting back in Oregon, that I will see her when I return.

One of the very few nonessential, non-hiking items I have been carrying in my backpack is what is called a chakra worry stone. It is a small, smooth oval that sits in the palm of your hand. There is an indentation for a thumb. You stroke it to, presumably, calm anxiety. It is a beautiful thing made of thin layers of red jasper, yellow jade, tigereye, green aventurine, sodalite, lapis lazuli, and amethyst. I have had it for years. I want to give it to Federico. His kindness and attentiveness have transformed this day for me. But I am selfish—I love this thing—and so I hesitate. I thank him and hug him for the dinner, for my clean, dry laundry, and I head off to sleep in the almost hospital-clean room I share with the Brit and Hans.

The next morning, early, I am in the lobby adjusting my backpack, getting ready to head off and find Kiki in the village a kilometer or two ahead. I am holding the worry stone in my hand. Federico comes from the back room to say goodbye. I hand him the stone. I have to. I think it belongs with him. I don't say anything, and neither does he. Then he grabs my hand, squeezes it, and asks me to wait. He goes into the back room and returns with a delicate, half-inch silver scallop shell, a charm, an amulet, the iconic symbol of the Camino. It has a tiny loop on top that will allow me to string through a cord and wear it as a necklace. When I get home, four weeks later, this is what I do. I am wearing the necklace now, as I write this.

13

THE CHORES HE DID. The life we lived. These were my thoughts one late-winter afternoon as I finished pruning the Anjou and moved on to the Hosui Asian pear, its next-orchard neighbor. I liked Asian pears more than he did. I liked a lot of things he didn't, from Brussels sprouts to backcountry hiking, from awakening at dawn to watching *House Hunters International*. And he liked Afghani food and cribbage and *Game of Thrones*. But, when he died four months before pruning time, we had been married for more than three decades and we had (mostly) made it work.

Pruning wasn't my chore. It had never been my chore. Neither had I been responsible for mowing the front meadow on the tractor. Or checking the propane level in the big tank on the side of the house. Or remembering that Tuesday was garbage day. But now, it was all me. I had watched Tom prune the trees every year for decades. But until I hefted the ladder from spot to spot, until I climbed up and down scores of times, until I started lopping off branches above my head, I didn't realize how hard it was. I was wearing Tom's barn jacket, warm, familiar, but too big and as filthy as a working jacket can be that had not been washed in twenty years. I reached into the pocket and found a balled-up tissue. Had I asked a forensic scientist, I would have been told that it still harbored "copious amounts" of his DNA.

We had moved out to this land eight years into our marriage. It was a shaggy five-acre plot of second- and third-growth Douglas fir and white oak with the usual western Oregon tangle of vine maple and invasive blackberry. We cleared an acre, built a house (rather, designed a house that others built for us), created a huge garden, planted an orchard, deer-fenced it against the marauders that Tom insisted on calling "rats with antlers," raised chickens, raised children, and created side-by-side careers as writers. We did what it took to make a place go, to make a marriage go. We were better, sometimes, with the former than with the latter.

When a garden needs weeding, you see it, you know it. You do it. You get down on your hands and knees and dig out those offenders by the roots. When the soil is depleted, it tells you, and you work in more compost, manure, bonemeal, lime. Fruit trees need pruning every year. You don't question this. You do it. Or rather, Tom did it. If you don't whack back the blackberries, they take over, so you whack. And you keep whacking. But a long marriage is different. Or for us it was.

A long marriage takes itself for granted. There is a line—I know there is, and I know we crossed it—between being at ease with someone, knowing that someone is there, counting on them—and taking them for granted, failing to see the specialness of what you have, failing to do the work to keep the specialness of what you *had*. A long marriage between two people who don't do things to hurt each other, who settle into what is often enough comfort, who learn to accommodate or keep their own counsel—that kind of marriage doesn't tell you what it needs. It just keeps on keeping on. And then you learn too late that what you ignored, or buried and then were too scared to excavate, what you refused to admit, what you learned to live with because really, everything was okay, wasn't it?—all that surfaces as regret. Or, to be honest, as anger.

Fifty percent of marriages end in divorce. Can that be right? It seems both too great a number—do half of couples who pledge "'til death do us part" part before death?—and too little. I know almost no one who has not been divorced. That was never going to happen with our marriage, and it did not. Marriages end because of infidelity or financial difficulties, substance abuse, domestic violence, or that vague and all-encompassing "irreconcilable differences." None of which applied to us. How many marriages end because people just stop paying attention?

The thing is, we parented well. We traveled together well. We took care of business well. We just didn't take care of our *own* business that well, our own emotional business. And now I know, although I didn't at the time, how and why and when that happened. Up here in the branches of the Fuji tree, clipping, lopping, shaping, thinking about what we had and what we didn't have, I know there are lessons to be learned and that these lessons transcend the marriage. This is a good place to learn them, or begin to.

The Fuji is the biggest tree in the orchard. The other trees are dwarfs. This one—our mistake at the nursery—is not and has over the years grown into a stately presence, a tree that provides shade, a tree you can sit under. Because it was Tom's favorite, I dug in some of his ashes around its base and then marked the spot with a cluster of stones. The Fuji is also the unruliest tree in the orchard. Before pruning, it looks like a big umbrella with spikes, the scores of spindly water sprouts growing straight up from mature branches that form its curved upper structure. There are suckers coming from the lower trunk, and inward-facing, crossover branches that make a tangle of the middle of the tree. The Fuji needs a major haircut, not just a trim. But I know from the instructional YouTubes I watched to make myself smart enough to take on this task that it is possible to be overzealous, to over-prune.

If you prune too many branches from a fruit tree, you can kill it. And even if the tree does not die, it will spend its energy producing more water sprouts that do not produce fruit. Over-pruning does the opposite of what you intended. It reduces harvest and weakens tree structure. And so, you prune carefully. You focus on the core integrity of the tree. Does it seem too precious to say that this horticultural knowledge sparks a nonhorticultural insight? That I realize that when I look up into the tree and see all that is "wrong," I am blinded to what is right: its strong trunk, its solid limbs, its longevity? Did I do that with my marriage, the last half, when the disconnects, the distances (the "wrongs," those water sprouts) blinded me to what was still so good? Clearly, that "tree" needed attention, it needed pruning. In choosing not to do this, not to do the work of consciously, actively making the marriage stronger, I think now I was afraid of "over-pruning." I think I was afraid that if I started down that path, there would be nothing left of us. The YouTube gardener says, "Over-pruning may even expose the tree's trunk and remaining branches to excessive sunlight, which can lead to sunscald and sunburn, ultimately proving fatal for the tree." Yes, that is what I thought.

But there is more to it than that. When you live with someone for most of your adult life, when you cycle through the stages of adulthood with someone, shit happens. And shit happened. Fourteen years into our marriage, living busy, vigorous, active lives, the house filled with lively, healthy children, then eleven, nine, and three years old, with two nascent literary careers and two serious full-time *don't-quit-your-day-job* professions, the orchard in full production, we had so much going right that we thought nothing would ever go wrong.

I went in for my yearly mammogram in the late spring. A week later, I got a call to come back in. The radiologist had "seen something." I had another mammogram. Reading the second scan, the radiologist deemed the "something" *worrisome.* I went in for a biopsy. Of all the things that were to happen in the next year and a half, one of my clearest memories is sitting in the waiting room of the surgeon's office, my legs and arms tightly crossed, holding myself together, seeking my own protection, seeking to take up as little space as possible, crying but trying to make no noise. There was one other woman in the waiting room, an "older" woman, maybe as old as I am now. She came over, sat down next to me, said nothing, and hugged me around the shoulders.

While I was waiting for the results of the biopsy, Tom had a stroke. I know. I know how that sounds. But that was the truth of it. He didn't fall down or stop speaking or become paralyzed. If any of that had happened, we would have reacted quickly. If he had been in his sixties rather than his mid-forties, if he had been in questionable health, if there had been a *watch-out-for-this* family history, we would have acted differently. But he was a hale and hearty guy who just got very dizzy and nauseated and said he felt weird. We thought it was a panic attack because of this *worrisome* "something," which it was hard to imagine was anything other than breast cancer, although neither of us had said this out loud.

He stumbled into bed. I scrounged around in the bathroom cabinet and found Dramamine and a bottle with a few almost-expired Xanax pills. He swallowed them and promptly threw up. I gave him another dose. Those stayed down, but the dizziness and otherworldly feelings remained. He stayed in bed. Finally, many hours later, near midnight, when nothing had changed, when we knew something must be very wrong, I called a neighbor to come over and stay with the sleeping children. Together, my neighbor and I held on to Tom and guided him down the stairs and into the car. We had a minivan back then. I laid him flat in the back and drove to the emergency room.

A blood clot had lodged itself in an artery in his cerebellum, that portion of the brain tucked under the cerebrum next to the brain stem that controls balance, standing, and other motor functions. This is what the doctors learned after CT scans and an MRI, an angiogram, an echocardiogram, and maybe other tests—blood, urine, vision, cognition—while they waited, and we waited, to see if the swelling in his brain would go down. Had

Google been around in the late '90s, I would have learned this: "Ischemic edema occurs within hours after stroke onset and is associated with an 80 percent mortality." What I knew then, what I was told, was that they were carefully monitoring "intracranial pressure," and if the swelling didn't start subsiding (thanks to whatever they were pumping into his system), they would "open the cranial vault" to relieve the pressure. They would, in other words, saw open his skull. If, one way or another, the swelling didn't go down, there would be permanent brain damage, most likely significant brain damage. No one said the word *death*, but I heard it.

Tom's oldest sister drove down from Portland to care for the kids. I spent all day at the hospital, not because there was anything I could do, and not because Tom was responsive—the medications, the continued extreme vertigo, robbed him of any ability to interact—but because what else was I supposed to do? I forgot about my worrisome mammogram and the biopsy results that were to come. I forgot that people's lives continued all around me. I did not forget the children. When I came home after visiting hours, I told them Daddy had a really bad headache and had to stay in the hospital for a few days, which wasn't really a lie. I assured them that all was okay, which felt very much like a lie, but it was the lie I had to tell.

Three days later, I got the biopsy report: invasive ductal carcinoma. It would be weeks before I understood what this meant, before I understood *stage* and *grade* and *receptors*, before I sat with an oncologist, a surgeon, a radiologist, before I drove 350 miles to get a second opinion. What I thought then was that I wouldn't be alive to see my older son make it through middle school. What I thought then was: I cannot tell anyone about this. I cannot tell Tom, lying semicomatose in a hospital bed. I cannot tell my sweet sister-in-law, who is taking care of the kids. I cannot tell my father-in-law, who drove down to spend time at his son's bedside. Their focus was and needed to be on Tom. It did not feel odd to have long conversations with Tom's family and not mention my news. I was protecting them. I was insulating myself. I did not have the emotional stamina to tell a friend. Or the time. About my own parents? I'm not sure I even gave them a thought. They knew so little about me. Why would I share this?

Toward the middle of day four, Tom's neurologist told me that the swelling had gone down enough for her to take skull-sawing off the agenda. By day five, the pressure inside his head was almost back to normal, and the crisis was deemed over. Tom was very weak. His head was pounding. He could not stand unassisted. He would need a lot of rest, and rehab, and he would need to be on blood-thinning medication for the rest of his life. But there would be a rest of his life. That late afternoon, I was walking back to his room after drinking bad coffee at the hospital cafeteria when one of his nurses stopped me in the hallway. "He's worried about you," she said. Apparently, there had been some bedside conversation. "You need to tell him what's going on." Tom knew about the worrisome mammogram, and he knew I had gone in for a biopsy, but results had come after his stroke, during his days in the hospital. I hadn't figured out a way—or a time—to tell him.

I don't remember what I said, how I presented the diagnosis. I do remember what I did not say: I did not say what I was thinking. I did not say I thought I was going to die. Mostly what I remember about that day, the day I knew Tom would make it, was rushing home, corralling the children, stopping to pick up a large pizza and taking the kids to see their father for the first time in almost a week. He was sitting up in bed. They hugged him. I laid out the pizza box across his lap. We got greasy fingers all over those crisp, white hospital sheets. Two days later, he was home. And we were a family again. It was late June with the rhodies blooming and the sky that cerulean blue that erases care, and I sat outside on the grass with Tom. And in the sunshine, in that moment, with this guy who could have died but didn't, I snapped out of it. "It" being the fear and self-pity that I had kept hidden from everyone (but myself). I had not seen a path forward. Now all I wanted to do was forge ahead. Maybe it was the sunshine. Maybe I am just not built for wallowing. It happened in an instant, surprising both Tom and me. I turned to him and said, "I'm gonna make it. I'm gonna be okay. We're gonna be okay."

And that was it. That was our pact. We had our separate battles, but we also had this united front. I thought of it as a battle then. And I was going to win with very few people knowing I was even engaged in a war.

When they unhooked me from the chemo drip that first time, I drove to a blueberry farm a few miles out of town and spent the next three hours picking in the afternoon sun. I monitored myself obsessively. Each minute that passed when I didn't feel weird or nauseous or tired gave me hope. I talked to myself a lot during those three hours. *See, this isn't so bad. You are strong. You can do this.* The chemo I chose—my cancer was so very common and so well studied that there were actually choices—omitted the "red devil" drug, the one that left you hairless. So through the treatment, the chemo and then the radiation, I looked like me. And because there is nothing that takes my appetite away, I did not lose weight. I masqueraded as a healthy person. I lived my life as a mother of three. I kept my teaching position at the university. I finished writing the manuscript for a book and submitted it on time. My editor had no idea I was undergoing treatment for cancer. It was a huge source of personal pride, this secret-keeping, this presenting as "normal," this "passing" as healthy. And then, within a year—a very long year—I did not have to pass anymore. I was healthy. As was Tom. But the war we had both fought had taken its toll.

These back-to-back, overlapping events were life-changing, but not in the way one would expect. Tom made a full recovery. He had no loss of memory or movement or function at all. The only lasting effect was that he had to take those blood thinners. "Rat poison," he called his daily doses. Because, actually, that's what warfarin is. And he had to go in once a month to have Nurse Bob test his blood viscosity to adjust, if necessary, his rat-poison dosage. I had to slog through more than a year of treatment that made me feel sicker than I ever felt during those few times in my life when I had actually been sick. That year went by in slo-mo, although now, remembering it, it seems like a blip. I kept my head down and my shoulder to the wheel. We told the children what we thought they needed to know. They never knew that Tom's brain could have swelled. They never knew their father could have died. They never knew that my cancer could have spread. They never knew they could have been orphans. They knew, we told them, that something serious had happened, but that we were fine, that life as they knew it, as we had all been living it, would continue.

The three of them moved through their paces: seventh grade, fifth grade, preschool. I was not happy—but the fact was that Tom was fine, and I was cured. Oncologists do not use that word. They say *in remission*, which, to those of us who've been down this path, feels ominous, as in: Watch out. That cancer is just waiting quietly in the wings, biding its time, ready to come back. But after a year, then five years—that gold standard "survival" rate—then a decade, and now almost three, I use the C-word (*cure*, not *cancer*) with confidence. I emerged from that year with a different body, but like Tom, I emerged healthy.

What did we do? When people go through something this big, they *do* something big. Don't they? We did not sell everything and move to a Greek island because we realized that life is precious and pledged to live every day as if it were our last. We did not renew our vows in front of family and friends in a big ceremony on a grassy meadow full of wildflowers. But life did change. It changed in big ways we did not recognize or acknowledge and therefore did not address or process. And, looking back, it seems to me that this is the moment our marriage lost something. This is when we pulled apart. Brené Brown, whose work I wouldn't start to read until many years later, nailed it when she wrote about the insidious "betrayal of disengagement," that moment of "letting the connection go."

What happened was that I armored myself during that year we were both recovering. I went to my first chemo treatment—all the treatments—solo. It was not an experience I wanted to share with anyone. If I was going to freak out, break down, or throw up, I preferred to do it with no one watching. The nurses had seen it all, so they didn't count. I didn't want solace. I didn't want pity. I wanted strength, and I felt then that the only source was myself.

I took pride in my ability to handle everything. It was, I see now, more hubris than pride. Not to mention ego. But it was necessary at the time because Tom wasn't there in those crucial days after the biopsy and after the diagnosis. And so, I just sucked it up. I began to see myself as even more self-reliant and independent than I already thought I was (which was a lot). I told myself that I needed no one. In fact, for a while, I had no one. Tom literally wasn't there. I couldn't count on him. I knew, of course, that it was not his fault that he was not there for me. But that didn't prevent me from feeling abandoned. On my own. No safety net. And thus, the armor. I see this all now. I did not see it then.

And then there was how we were together, two wounded warriors who had won our separate battles. We were so proud of our bounce-back to good health, so very proud that we shielded the children from the awfulness of what had happened. We, the two of us, went through the storm and survived and powered on. We didn't talk about it. We were just so relieved to be through it, to be back to our lives. But we weren't back to what we had. Not really.

We were changed, fundamentally. What happened later, and there was a lot of "later"—two decades more of marriage—came from my armoring and his turning ever inward. And it came from our lack of attention to what we had been through together. The experience, if fully felt, if shared emotionally, could have strengthened us. Instead, first because of how we felt we needed to present ourselves—both to each other and to the children—during his months of recovery and my year of treatment, and then because of the distance we felt between us but did not acknowledge, and then because of the awkwardness of talking across that distance, and then because too much time had elapsed and we forgot how to talk to each other . . . what happened was we lost some of what we had built together. And it would take his illness, that final year, for us to have a sense of that. And by then, there was too much else, so much else, to think about and plan for and work through and get through that there was almost no room for us. "I didn't realize how much I loved you," Tom said to me during the last week of his life. We were sitting up side by side on his narrow hospital bed in the living room. That was all that was said, all that could be said.

14

ONE TIME, IN THE middle of the night, maybe 3:00 a.m., Lizzie texted me. She had gotten to work at the bakery more than an hour late, which was, we were beginning to see, becoming the norm. This bad habit had not yet caught up with her. She worked alone, and as long as she fulfilled all the orders by the time the place opened for business, no one was the wiser. But this night, there were more orders, many more dozens of bagels and muffins to bake than on previous shifts. She was overwhelmed and frazzled. She needed my help. *She was asking for my help.* I could help her solve a momentary crisis. That's a clean and beautiful thing, an uncomplicated transaction, a gift, like in the simple days of childhood when a parent has the magical powers of solving problems, when problems were little blips and not the tip of some dangerous, unseen iceberg. I drove into town and worked with her, side by side. She bossed me around. She had to. I didn't know my way around those industrial machines, those cauldrons, those massive ovens. We worked until dawn. That night, I had an enormous appreciation for not just the skill but the physicality of what she did. This was really hard work. No wonder she was tired all the time. No wonder she was moody. No wonder she was becoming increasingly hard to live with. It was the job. It was the topsy-turvy life.

She was eighteen, a high school graduate, working long shifts and half-heartedly attending classes at the local community college, dropping out one term, returning another, ping-ponging between enthusiasm and boredom, one day imagining working for a crisis hotline, the next talking about opening up a food cart downtown. She could work in eldercare. She could develop and market her own line of cookies. With every new idea, every sizzle and pop of creative energy, she would come alive, and Tom and I would nod encouragingly and ask (what we thought were) supportive questions and jump in with (what we thought were) helpful suggestions. Maybe parental approval is a death knell. That could have been part of what was happening. But it was also, I think, just the way she was, a personality trait.

My mother was the same way: a dreamer, not a doer; long on ideas, short on follow-through. Many enthusiasms. No plan. During the last of Lizzie's three lackluster quarters at the community college, she came home gushing about this one teacher she had for a counseling psych course, and how she could see herself doing this work, and how important this was. And then, halfway through the term, she forgot her notebook at school, and couldn't find it, and never reached out to the teacher to tell her what had happened, and stopped going to class. I told myself this was just part of her mercurial nature, that she was slow to bloom into adulthood. She needed to make these mistakes, Tom said, and she would learn from them. He was sure of it. It did not occur to me, to us, then that she might have already begun her descent into drugs. She smoked weed. Big deal. Everyone smoked weed. This was Oregon.

Then she was nineteen, with no plans other than whom she might meet up with before work or where the Saturday kickball game would be held. She was working longer shifts at another bakery, a better bakery, living the upside-down life of a graveyard-shift worker, which meant in at midnight, out at eight. This post–high school life, with Lizzie in her childhood room with its shelves of Beanie Babies and its bookcase full of middle school track-and-field trophies and Beverly Cleary paperbacks, was a time warp. Did she feel it, or was it just me?

We—Lizzie, Tom, and I—were in transition as a family. But none of us knew what we were transitioning to. Our two sons had gone to college, and those transitions were tough; the letting-go was painful, the fabric of the family had to be rewoven, but we were traveling well-worn paths. With Lizzie, it was different. She was at home, but she wasn't. We rarely saw her. She didn't eat meals with us. A curfew was nonsensical because of her work schedule and because she was nineteen. And who gives a nineteen-year-old a curfew? And what nineteen-year-old would pay attention? Occasionally, and then more than occasionally, she wouldn't come home for days. She'd text that she had gone over to someone's house after work, and then fallen asleep on a couch there, and then gotten up and gone to work. Or maybe, on a day off, her kickball pals had gone from the field to the dive bar to someone's house, where she'd fallen asleep on the couch. There was, in those days, a lot of couch-sleeping. There was this narrative she was spinning—and I think sometimes it was true—that she was being responsible by not coming home. She was too tired to drive. Or she'd been drinking. She was just being safe.

And then, for no reason we could discern, things would change again, and she would be home more often, and she would want to cook a dinner for us, and she would ask if she could come to the gym with me, and Tom would look at me and nod. *You see, I told you she'd find her way.* During one of those periods, she asked if she could bring home a guy she had started seeing. We did not know then that he was the deadbeat dad of her extravagantly tattooed and multipierced older friend's first child. We did not know that he had spent time in juvenile detention for setting fire to a dumpster behind a store. What we knew is that Lizzie wanted to introduce him to us, and that was enough.

He came for dinner. It is difficult now to admit that I liked him at that first encounter. I remember that he seemed at ease with us, which is an extraordinary feat when meeting your girlfriend's parents for the first time. I remember that he and Tom conversed about science subjects, and although he seemed maybe a little too sure of himself—going head-to-head with my husband on any science subject was an act of bravery, or arrogance—he also appeared to be well read and curious about the world around him. I remember Lizzie looking over at the two of them, listening but probably not really listening, just pleased to see her father's engagement, his perceived approval. This is what I remember. I also may have been momentarily blinded to who he was because he seemed better than the last guy she brought home: a mumbler, awkward, smelling of beer and cigarettes. I wanted this one to be different. And so, I don't trust my memory. I need independent verification. I need fact-checking. I ask Jackson, my older son, what he remembered about FA. They had met a few times. He doesn't hesitate: "Greasy, tired, hungover, off-putting." But then, his memory is colored by what came after.

Lizzie moves in with Jackson, a move we all endorse. It feels like a step forward. He's living in town, in an old house we've spent time rehabbing as a family project. He's working full-time and has a lovely girlfriend. Lizzie is working her graveyard shifts, hanging out with her collection of kickball and dive-bar friends, and more and more becoming a part of the life FA leads. Because she's not living at home—and because her brother stays out of her business—Tom and I don't know that she is in fact living at FA's. But slowly, over the course of a few months, we begin to learn the circumstances of this life. It begins when she comes home late one afternoon, pale and weary, carrying a huge trash bag full of dirty clothes. That's what kids do, bring their laundry with them on visits. But the house we thought she was living in with her brother has a washer and dryer in the basement, so why would she be lugging this bag home? And the clothes? Many of them are FA's, a collection of torn jeans and death metal shirts.

She looks so very tired, my girl, and her beautiful, thick, light brown hair is lank and greasy. She goes upstairs and takes a very long shower. Then I feed her something, I don't remember what, and she attacks it like she hasn't eaten in days. I don't ask her anything. When I ask is when the wall goes up, and the defenses are fortified. I let her eat. I sit there. Hesitatingly at first, then in a rush, she tells me about FA's house, a one-bedroom "shack"—her word—with a single space heater to warm the place, mold along the baseboards, a leak under the kitchen sink. "I'm going to help him fix it up," she tells me. She is excited about this. What I know she (also) means is *I'm going to fix him up*. She tells me that FA hasn't held down a job in several years, that his parents (his father is a physician; they live in a McMansion neighborhood in town) support him by paying the rent on the place and giving him a weekly stipend as long as he stays "clean." She says he used to shoot heroin but doesn't anymore. She says he drinks, a lot, and smokes weed. I wonder how the father checks on him. I wonder what the father knows. I wonder what the father does not want to know.

I know that what I say next will not change anything, but I have to say it. I tell her to get out of there, that this is an unhealthy place for her to be, that she is harming herself more than she can ever help him. I plead with her to move back to her older brother's house, or to this house. She has choices. She has options. She doesn't want to hear any of this. She may not, in fact, be listening. I can see it in how she stiffens. She pushes back the chair, stuffs the clothes from the dryer into the plastic garbage sack, and leaves. The next time I see her, maybe two weeks later, she has a black eye and a split lip. She tells me a funny story about doing a face-plant after tripping over one of the legs of the spiral dough mixer at the bakery. I know that machine. I can imagine the scene. We laugh together.

Three weeks later, she calls from the ER. She has a cracked rib, a fractured lumbar vertebra, and contusions on her arms and legs. She tells me the truth this time, or rather, she tells me part of the truth: FA pushed her up against a wall and punched her so hard that she fell to the floor. And then he kicked her. He was wearing boots. We don't find out the whole story until, a harrowing year later, I read the handwritten report for the restraining order she files against him. Does it help to know the awful statistics? That my daughter is one of the one in four women who are victims of what the National Coalition Against Domestic Violence calls "severe intimate partner physical abuse." That she is the prime demographic: Women between the ages of eighteen and twenty-four are the most commonly abused? And what do I do with the information I glean from this research, this research that places my daughter in such a harrowing context, this research that links physical trauma, from which she will heal, to the embedded traumas, the anxiety, hypertension, PTSD, and a higher risk of developing addictions to drugs and alcohol associated with abuse?

She goes from the ER back to his house. *She goes back to him.* And as we learn later, after we strong-arm her into filing a police report, after he is taken into custody, the physical and psychological abuse has been part of this relationship for almost as long as there has been a relationship. She has kept this hidden. She has stayed. And now, even after visible harm, even after an incident so severe that she took herself to the ER, she has returned.

Tom talks to her about therapy, although he does not use that word. "It would be good for you to talk to someone," he tells her. He treads so lightly. I admire his restraint. When he talks, she seems to listen. I research the therapists in town, looking for a youngish woman who works with domestic-abuse victims. I hand Lizzie a list. She makes promises. She tells us what we want to hear. Nothing comes of it. I try to get her to talk about the relationship, refraining from the language that didn't work the last time, trying to reframe the conversation so she doesn't see it as criticism about her choices. Which of course it is. But it is also my desire to understand, my deep confusion, my sense that if only I did understand, I could help. She tells me that he is sorry that he hurts her, that he knows he "needs help," that he promises to be better. He is so, so sorry, she says. And she believes him.

I read about the four-stage cycle of abusive relationships, which goes like this: First, tension building, during which the abuser displays regular bouts of anger, and the victim becomes hypervigilant, doing everything she can to appease, to avoid a bigger blowup. Second, the incident, or incidents, often a combination of threats as well as acts of violence. Third, the reconciliation phase, during which the abuser does everything to win back trust—apologies, gifts, promises to change—or turns the table on the victim, making her believe that what happened is her fault. Lizzie said something like this to me when I asked her to tell me about the beating itself. She blamed herself for "making him mad." And then there is calm, the final stage when the victim, my daughter, believes things might be changing. The calm gives the victim an opportunity to forget what has happened, to erase the past. And then it begins again.

I don't detail these stages for her. That's lecturing. That's me, know-it-all mother, telling her I can make more sense out of her life than she can. But I ask her to think about the idea that relationships have cycles and that sometimes it is up to someone to break the unhealthy ones. I tell her how much I believe in her. And then I do my own deep dive into why women stay in abusive relationships. If Lizzie can't tell me, or if she doesn't know, maybe those who study this can help me.

I find a disturbing and fascinating piece of research based on an analysis of almost seven hundred Twitter postings following a highly publicized case of domestic abuse by an NFL player. The women responded by detailing their own stories of abuse. The researchers coded the responses and identified eight themes that ran through these stories. The first three, it seems to me, speak directly to my daughter's experience. "Distorted thoughts" is about the confusion, doubts, and self-blame that come from being controlled and traumatized. Women wrote about being ashamed and embarrassed, about blaming themselves for triggering their abuser. Lizzie said as much to me. Then there is "wanting to be a savior," which is the leitmotif of her life, the foundation for almost every friendship she has had from middle school on. "I believed I could love the abuse out of him," one woman wrote. I got chills reading that. "Damaged self-worth" is a third theme, the result of degrading treatment within the relationship but also, probably, the self-image or self-talk a woman might have brought to the relationship in the first place.

I have done much work around negative self-talk myself. I don't know any woman who does not have—and has not worked to silence—that *I am not ______ enough* voice in her head. There's a vast cottage industry devoted to this, so many books and podcasts and retreats and seminars. So much advice. But to work on something, you must recognize and acknowledge it. If only she would agree to therapy. Tom tries again. And again. Then backs off as her resistance stiffens, as he sees, as we both see, that this just feeds into her *I'm not ______ enough* self-talk. There is one other reason these women cite that I think I, and our family, can do something about: isolation. Manipulative partners, the research indicates, try to separate the victim from family and friends. Living on the other side of town from us, alternately working graveyard shifts and sleeping odd hours, living whatever life is unfolding in that shack, Lizzie is far from us. We must get her back.

It is her boss at the bakery who steps in. FA is now showing up at her workplace at three or four in the morning. There is shoving and hitting, yelling. The boss does not see this. What he sees is Lizzie is missing her quotas. He sees quality declining. He tells her she is in jeopardy of losing the job. The next time FA shows up at her work and pushes her around, she calls the police. Tom and I had been pressing her to do this after the ER visit, but she resisted. The cops come and haul him away, housing him in the county jail. Lizzie is interviewed. She files a report. I am so very proud of her. And I am also mortified that this is happening within our family. But FA is in jail, and Lizzie is at home. That's what counts. The case goes to trial. Lizzie is not required to be there. FA is found guilty of strangulation, assault in the fourth degree, and menacing, for which he receives a ninety-day sentence. Yes, ninety days. And he gets credit for the two weeks he spent awaiting his day in court. Post-jail, he will be on thirty-six months of probation.

How I would love this to be the end.

It is not the end.

He is released. He begins texting and calling Lizzie. He persuades some young woman to give him a ride out to our property and then sends her walking down the access road to our house with a message for Lizzie to meet him up by the street. Tom is furious. He marches up the road and finds FA standing by the mailbox. I know, because he tells me, how much my husband wants to inflict bodily harm. But, of course, he doesn't. He orders FA off the property and threatens him with more legal action. Lizzie is upstairs asleep. When she awakens, Tom tells her what happened. Then he writes her a note. I do not see the note until two years later when I find it in a box Lizzie kept, stacked in the storage unit I clean out after her death. This is what is says, in part:

> *If he loves you, he needs to recognize the damage he is doing, face up to his issues, and get serious about changing. He needs to stop bullshitting and get started. It breaks my heart when I see you losing your life, your health, your self-respect. I think you had great hopes of helping FA. Instead, he is dragging you down. . . .*
>
> *What happens now is up to you. Listen again, Lizzie: It's up to you. Your choices got you into this situation, and you are going to have to make some choices to get out of it. I know you can do that. Any time you're ready to make a positive move, we are behind you 100%. You're strong and proud, but never be too proud to ask for help.*

He concludes with another plea for her to seek professional help. And, of course, with *I love you.*

A day after Tom's encounter with him by the mailbox, I get this email from FA with the subject line: "Please don't hate me."

> *I am aware of your and your husband's feelings toward me. I have been struggling with BPD and am working toward recovery every day.*

I have to google *BPD*. It can stand for either *bipolar disorder* or *borderline personality disorder*. He has a mental illness? Which one? If bipolar, then he cycles through periods of mania and depression. But intense emotional instability is also a hallmark of borderline personality disorder. If this is what he suffers from, he would experience—and Lizzie would be directly affected by—rapid and intense mood swings, impulsivity, and risky behaviors. Has he, in fact, been diagnosed, or is he just throwing around terms? He is in treatment? He is "working toward recovery"? This is all news to us. Is this part of the way he manipulates my daughter, by presenting his anger and abuse as part of a mental illness?

> *I do have relapses and I do everything in my power to recognize my triggers and discover coping skills to modify my actions.*

He certainly has the language down. Does it come from doing the work, or is it bullshit?

> *I wish to sincerely apologize for my unacceptable outbursts of anger. I do love and cherish your daughter very much and am personally disgusted by my actions on the occasions where I lose control. . . . I hope to be able to see Liz again very soon,* ***seeing there is no legal order barring us from being together at this time.***

The boldface is mine. I read this as aggressive, a direct pushback against Tom banishing him from the property, a statement of his future intentions. I also interpret the apology as an expression of the third stage of the abusive relationship cycle I read about, that period when the abuser does everything to win back trust. He ended the email to me with this:

> *I understand she needs time to process this past year. . . . Thank you for raising an amazing young woman.*

I read that last sentence with more anger than I thought I had in me, thinking, *Would that be the "amazing woman" to whom you gave a black eye, a split lip, multiple bruises, a fractured vertebra, and a cracked rib? The amazing woman you kicked with your boots?* I cannot know the truth of FA's mental health. I can see only his actions. And Tom and I can very clearly read that, regardless of him being forbidden on our property, he will make contact with Lizzie. And, if the past year is any indication, regardless of his uncontrolled anger and violence, our daughter will find her way back to him.

15

MY PONYTAIL SLAPS MY face; the grit of the road dermabrades my skin. I smell of sweat and diesel, and I want to be done with it. I want to be anywhere but here trudging in the heat. The Camino, on this unlovely stretch, is a hard dirt path that skirts the highway close enough so the gusts created by the semis that zip by whip at my hair. Kiki and I power right past the albergue where we intend to stay tonight. We don't even notice the place. That's because it's on the other side of the N120, a busy two-lane national road we've been following most of the day.

We walk almost two kilometers past the albergue before we realize our mistake. It's not just the heat and the highway and the long day. It's that this albergue, when we find it by backtracking and then sprinting across the busy highway, does not look like an albergue. It is a three-story, square redbrick building sitting behind a triple row of gas pumps. Parked at the pumps are three semis and four delivery vans. This is a truck stop.

Of all the lessons of the Camino, the hardest to learn is the least complicated: What you count on one day disappears the next, and sometimes that's good, and sometimes that is not so good, but you keep going. If there's a trick to it, it's to allow yourself to be charmed while knowing how quickly charm fades. If there's a trick to it, it is learning how to stay alert but not anxious, how to be both grounded and nimble. The Camino is about cultivating the ability to move from one unknown to another. I think about this a lot. I am moving from wife to widow, from mother of three to mother of two. Or maybe I am just moving.

Five days ago, I walked west through quiet farmland, my back to a lemony dawn, feeling weightless and free. I had washed the dust of the Meseta from my clothes and my hair. The long trek across the arid plateau was past. That afternoon, I had sat next to Kiki in a sun-dappled ancient church courtyard in the presence of quietly rapturous nuns and weary but blissed-out pilgrims, declaring why I was walking. It was the most perfect, the most cinematic, of moments. And yet, now that I deconstruct it, it was not as simple, not as perfect. It was burdened with lessons to attend to. That afternoon, just a few days ago, I had said—and I was being honest—that I had chosen to come to Spain to walk the five hundred miles of the Camino because I needed to do something big to separate the life I had been living from the life, the unknown life, the unexplored territory, that lay ahead of me. What I didn't say—because how do you say something like this in a church courtyard with beatific nuns and high-on-life backpackers from around the world—how do you say: I am walking because I am angry? How do you say, aloud, that you are furious about working so hard, for so long, to create a life that had, in a literal heartbeat, in two heartbeats, vanished? How do you say that grief is expected and acceptable? It is insistent but quiet. It whispers. If you are able to talk about grief, it's okay to talk about it. People understand. They say they understand.

But anger is something else. Anger is a storm that thrashes at you. How do you say that you are walking because you are angry about everything—disease, addiction, death, casual cruelties, systemic malice, American politics, everything—and that you are weary of wearing your anger like a blanket? The blanket protects, but it also smothers. How do you say any of this in a church courtyard? And so, I had said what I said, and felt underneath what I felt and left that unsaid, and I sang, and cried, and looked at the faces of the nuns. And in that moment, the blanket, I now realize, slipped off my shoulders just a little. I think it was the nuns, especially that younger one who sat in the middle, the one with the luminescent skin, the one whose small hands lay motionless on her lap atop the folds of her habit. This, also, is a lesson of the Camino that translates directly to life: that occasionally and gloriously, there are true aha moments, but mostly there is the long slog toward making sense of who you are.

The next day, the trail wends its way through acres and acres of hay, wheat, and sunflowers long harvested. This is not the Meseta, but still the color palette is buff and tan, tawny fields with gentle brown hills at the horizon. There are very few villages. The monotony is soothing until it isn't, until the need for a café con leche takes over, and this is all I can think of. And there is nothing but spent fields and a dirt trail until, in the late morning, a blip on the lonely landscape turns out to be a tiny food truck parked by the side of the path. There has been nothing for six miles. I know this is not magic. I know I didn't manifest this food cart. But there it is.

That night, I wonder about this *Camino provides* idea, this notion I've either dismissed or scoffed at many times on this journey. Maybe now, after several weeks—after those radiant nuns, after that openhearted owner of the Oasis albergue, after the almost ghostly appearance of the food truck—maybe there is something to this. The Camino has offered so much already, blasted me with its contrasts, providing me not just with the time to think and not think, not just with the luxury of silence and anonymity but with the opposite. In these few weeks of walking, I have, paradoxically, spent more time in my own company than ever before and have also encountered a greater assortment of humans than ever before. All these people, observed on the trail, encountered at a café, snoring next to me in an albergue dorm, Joan and her grace, Emily and her sweetness, Harry and his arrogance, my Frenchman and his...well, my Frenchman, and Kiki—part raunch, part literary sophistication—they are helping me home in on what I truly value in others: quirkiness, compassion, humility, humor. They are helping me see, more clearly than perhaps I want to, what I have lost. Maybe, I think in those moments of elation and lightness, they are inching me toward something. I am not sure what.

That night, Kiki and I swat flies from our better-than-it-needs-to-be pilgrims' meal in a café—the only place to get dinner—in the crumbling isolated hill town of Moratinos. There are more flies here than people, which is no exaggeration not only because there are more flies here than I have ever seen anywhere but because the population of this village is sixty-six, plus or minus. A recent census identifies one-fifth of the population as either octo- or nonagenarians, so you never know. It appears that all these elderly folks are walking their little dogs back and forth on the narrow calle that runs in front of the café.

Inside, the scene is lively, not just because of the commotion created by the half dozen diners slapping and whacking at flies with rolled-up menus but because of James. James is a handsomely grizzled, aging hippie, an Irishman who "discovered" this town fifteen years ago on the first of his many Caminos. He left his wife and several children behind and, according to the obviously oft-told tale he spins for this small, captive audience in the café, he never looked back. He is in his sixties and very drunk, but the kind of drunk a person who really knows how to drink is drunk. He is a veteran inebriated raconteur. He makes himself the center of attention with practiced ease, working the crowd—a discomfited couple from Australia; a very tall, very thin techie from Silicon Valley; the marginally amused café owner; a young woman who can't take her eyes off him; Kiki; and me. He is table-hopping, backslapping, performing magic tricks, drinking. Twice he calls over to Claire, the entranced young woman, a lovely twentysomething nurse from the UK who has fallen hard for his charms, to go into the café kitchen and bring out another bottle of wine. James and Claire, by virtue of their nightly patronage here, have the run of the place.

And so, it appears the Camino provides once again, but in a different way: It provides James with a stage, a new audience every night, cases of two-euro-a-bottle vino tinto, and an adoring woman. It provides Claire with an adventure she never imagined (and Kiki and I believe she will regret). She and James have plans to "fix up"—beyond an understatement—the crumbling stone building he purchased for a few thousand euros fifteen years ago. It sits less than a hundred feet from the café and has no roof, no windows, no electricity, no running water. Claire has planted a little garden in front. Kiki and I admire it—the garden, not the rubble of a building—as we walk from the café to our albergue.

Because this trek, this pilgrimage, is all about contrasts and pivots, about savoring but then letting go, the boisterous James-orchestrated adventure in "Fly Town" is followed by a quiet day of walking through sleepy villages, and then a full-moon predawn hike that brings me back to a soft green landscape with purple mountains ringing the horizon, and finally a full day in a glorious city, León. It is a city of cobblestone streets and Gothic architecture, the skyline dominated by the Catedral de León, a masterpiece of (Kiki informs me) the mid-thirteenth century with more spires, towers, and flying buttresses than you can count, and 1,800 square meters of stained glass. There are convents, basilicas, palaces, parks, plazas, and the remains of first-century Roman walls. There is, most notably, the Museo Casa Botines, a castle-like structure designed by Gaudí and devoted to his personal and professional history. This is first on Kiki's must-visit list. After finding our accommodations, off-loading our packs, and changing into flip-flops, we spend hours roaming the building. As with my rest day in Burgos, which now seems like ancient history—but was in fact exactly a week ago—I effortlessly morph into a tourist. There is café con leche on every corner. I sit in my third café of the day writing notes in my cuaderno, watching people, nursing my coffee. There is music in the background, and I recognize it with a start; it is Levon Helm singing an iconic Band song, "The Weight," and I tear up because in this moment I both miss and hate my country furiously and in equal measure. I tear up because I want to go home, and I never want to go home. I tear up because I think the weight is all on me. Outside on the street, the women are wearing high heels and scarlet lipstick.

And now, leaving León behind, after a long, hot, diesel-scented day of walking by the N120, Kiki and I have arrived at what we immediately refer to as "the truck stop albergue." The downstairs public space is a diner populated by truck drivers playing cards, the small tables littered with bottles of Estrella Galicia. The check-in for our room is at the bar. This place offered only private rooms, no dorms, so Kiki and I reserved a double for ourselves. We thought this would be a real treat. We heft our bodies and our backpacks up the back steps to our room on the third floor. The walls are painted a sickly yellowish brown. Either that or the walls had been white, and smokers over the years have managed to alter the color. The room has two narrow iron beds, no lamp, one outlet, and a grimy window that faces out to the gas pumps. We inspect it, laughing, because what else can we do? In one corner of the room, the baseboard is missing—it looks as if it has been ripped off—and the damage has been repaired by layers of now frayed duct tape. We have our own bathroom—a private bathroom!—but there is something strange about the door. Someone has gouged out around the cheap locking door-knob, probably with a flathead screwdriver, making a ragged hole in the door, one of the hollow-core doors where you can see the "stuffing." We stand in front of it and spin various horror stories. I think of the hotel room in the Coen brothers' movie *Barton Fink*: surreal, eerie, with an overlay of existential dread. That's this room. Then I fill the tiny bathroom tub with water, perch myself on the edge, soak my feet, and binge-eat a box of Trias Double Chocolate Triangle Cookies that I had crammed in my backpack a few days before. That's fifteen cookies.

An hour later, just time enough to experience a sugar high and the accompanying metabolic plummet, I am downstairs in the diner with Kiki, sitting at the only table not occupied by the truck drivers. We order our nine-euro-complete-with-wine dinner, and while Kiki makes use of the free Wi-Fi, I amble over to one of the tables by the window. These guys—all stout, middle-aged men wearing jackets featuring company logos—are having such a good time. Whatever card game they are playing involves more joking, teasing, table-knocking, and backslapping than the laying down or grouping of cards. They scribble bets on the back of a napkin, add up numbers, tease one another. I stand and watch for a moment, then ask permission to take their picture. They think this is the funniest thing ever. This place may be listed in my trusty camino.ninja app as an albergue, but from the warm and surprised reception I am getting from these guys, it seems very few pilgrims stay here. The men want me to join them—they will teach me the game—but I see that our dinner has arrived.

I have settled into the weird rhythm of this place. It is not what I expected and not what I wanted. Upstairs, our room is scary. The road noise is loud. But here, downstairs, there is laughter and lively chatter, camaraderie, a window into the real, non-Camino life of this country I am walking through. I connect to Wi-Fi to post an image of the card-playing truck drivers. Then I check my email. There is a message with an attachment from the state medical examiner's office. I stare at it. I know what it is. Sixteen weeks to the day since Lizzie died, one day short of the first anniversary of Tom's death, I am receiving my daughter's autopsy report. If I don't look at it, I will think about it obsessively. If I do look at it, I will be heartbroken.

I look at it.

16

ON THE FIFTEENTH OF October, my twenty-second day of walking across Spain, the dawn is dazzling. Granted, dawn is often a magical time, especially on the Camino when you take to the path in the dark and walk as the sky lightens, not knowing what is in store for you this day but knowing that it has begun. I have walked into such dawns. I have marveled at such dawns. But this one is different. The sky is periwinkle. The clouds are tangerine and apricot and honey seen through a sunlit jar. Ripe peach. Amber with tints of rose. The clouds are not big and billowy, nor are they thin and wispy. They are eddies and swirls, tufts, drifts, and veils, the shape, the configurations changing faster than I can keep track. The colors too. When did that apricot deepen into orange sherbet? How did I miss that periwinkle sky lightening to powder blue?

Emerson once wrote, "Nature always wears the color of the spirit." In that essay, he also notes—unnecessarily, I think—that nature inspires reverence, that its beauties are owned by nobody, and that most people, once they pass childhood, never really see nature. That is not me. That is not now. I put down my backpack and stand by the side of the dirt path, looking east across acres of spent sunflowers. I hurry to capture images on my phone. Then I rummage through the pack to find my cuaderno to scribble down the colors I am seeing before they disappear. A few pilgrims pass. One asks if I am okay.

I am, and I am not.

I knew, many months ago, that I did not want to be at home on this day, the first anniversary—if such a word can be used for this—of Tom's death. I could not wake up on this day in the bed we shared, sit drinking coffee at the beautiful old kitchen table we found in the back room of a secondhand store decades ago, look out over the meadow he mowed wearing his favorite filthy ball cap. I knew, from the moment of his death, that October 15 would be a day, for many years to come, maybe forever, that I would have to plan for. I learned quickly to prepare for these Grief Moments, these official markers: the one-week-ago marker, one month ago, six months, the first Thanksgiving without, the first Christmas without, his birthday, Father's Day, our wedding anniversary. I developed a ritual: I toasted him with a Negroni; I rested my palm on his mesa, the woven cloth bundle that held the rocks he collected; I sat under the Fuji tree with his buried ashes. I read Mary Oliver's "In Blackwater Woods": *when the time comes to let it go / to let it go*. I powered up the Ridgeline trail into the forest, pounding that grief, that anger, that I-don't-know-what into the earth with each footfall. I had a plan. In preparing like this, in planning, you can talk yourself into a place where the pain does not come as a surprise. You can armor yourself. Maybe "you" is not right here. Maybe other grievers don't do this, would not think this way. Maybe those "how to grieve" books that I have never read and will never read have opinions about such a strategy. But this is what I learned to do, early on. It is the surprise moments that stab your heart. My heart.

One morning a few weeks before I left for this trip, I was sitting on the floor with Henry, my grandson, who was then fourteen months old. I listened to him recite the names of all the people in his life, the names he now knew, the people he loved and trusted. Until recently, he had been a listener. Now he was a talker. And so, he pointed at me and said, "Wowo," which is me, Lolo. His *L*s are not quite there yet. And he said *Dada* and *Mama*. And then he said *Gamma*, who is his other grandmother, and *Papa*, who is his grandfather. And then, bam, it hit me: He had no other grandfather. And someday, when people ask him about his family, he will say, "I never knew my father's father. He died when I was just an infant."

I wondered in that moment what Henry would have called Tom. (Later, I learned that Zane, my younger son and Henry's father, and Liza, Henry's mother and my adored daughter-in-law, created memories for his child about the man named "Grandpa Tom." He also, this son of mine, talked about Aunt Lizzie and her place in our family.) I never doubted what kind of a grandfather Tom would have been. I knew. He would have delighted in this child as he delighted in our children. He would have loved him quietly, unself-consciously and unconditionally as he did our children. He would have read to him—with funny accents and quirky voices—sang songs, played the piano, planted pumpkins for him in the garden, alerted him to the birds swooping around the backyard feeder, occasionally bored him with scientific facts, watched him, with an open heart, as this child learned about the world, as this child became a boy, a man. Tom would have been an extraordinary grandfather. Of course, I had thought about this before, felt the sorrow of this before, but sitting on the floor playing with Henry, listening to him speak the names of his family: This was an unshielded moment. And I was flattened.

Other unplanned-for moments have been less freighted, pedestrian even: That time I almost lost it in the aisle of Whole Foods when, triggered by a display of canned chickpeas—*canned chickpeas*—I remembered that thrown-together dinner we made during an ice storm that cut power to the house. Or that time I was scanning my bookshelf and saw the spine of the book *Get Shorty*, which made me think of our first cat, who just showed up at the house one day and stayed. It was the first house we lived in together, tiny, drafty, old. We wrote side by side on a hollow-core door supported by two file cabinets. We loved the house. It was the beginning of us. We named the cat Chili, after Chili Palmer in the Elmore Leonard novel. Or that time I discovered a tall, thin, almost empty bottle of Björk, a woodsy, sweet Icelandic liqueur, on the back of a high shelf only Tom could reach and remembered the fire we tended on a patch of land under the green glow of the northern lights.

I think grief is like riding a roller coaster blind, not knowing, not being able to anticipate, the ups and downs. But then it's also like a dream you drop in and out of, with long moments of amnesia during which everything feels "normal" until, boom, a nightmare. Or maybe the experience of grief is closest to the lyric Robert Hunter wrote so many years before Tom and I even knew the other existed: "Sometimes the light's all shinin' on me / Other times I can barely see."

What I knew about this day, October 15, was that I didn't want to be at home, and I didn't want to be sideswiped. I needed to prepare. The Camino was part of that plan, although I did not know exactly where I would be on this day or how it might unfold. I certainly didn't anticipate the most breathtaking dawn I had ever been awake to see.

"It is a serious thing just to be alive on this fresh morning in this broken world," Mary Oliver wrote. I think about that as the day unfolds. It is a thirty-five-kilometer trek from Villadangos del Páramo, site of the glad-it's-in-the-rearview-mirror truck stop albergue, to Astorga. I am walking alone today. I need to be alone. Kiki and I will meet up later at day's end. The walk is arduous. The effort takes over. The physical labor nearly obliterates thought. Midmorning, I walk across a long, stone medieval bridge that spans a small river to find myself in yet another charming village. This one can trace its lineage back to 400-something CE and includes a fanciful history, perhaps accurate, concerning an epic jousting tournament that may or may not have taken place on this very bridge. On the main street, which is also the Camino itself, there is what appears to be a small café. It is café con leche time, so I off-load my pack, place it outside along a line of others, and enter. It turns out that the small café opens to a huge backyard meadow with little tables and dozens of wildly colorful pheasants and chickens wandering, showing off their extravagant plumage, pecking at the ground, approaching fearlessly for handouts, and posing for pictures that will show up seconds later in Instagram feeds. I am now so accustomed to this juxtaposition between an iconic ancient pilgrimage through medieval towns and modern-day pilgrims with smartphones uploading images across social media that it is no longer jarring, or ironic, or even noteworthy. The birds are noteworthy, though—turquoise, scarlet, garish gold, fiery orange red—even more startling than the sunrise of a few hours before. The coffee is not bad either.

The rest of the day is the extraordinary ordinariness of the Camino: the monotony of putting one foot in front of another, the quiet, the slowness of time. During the sporadic moments of thought that pop up between the long periods of no-thought, I consider the privilege of being *alive* to do this. I am alive, and he is not, and she is not, which is, of course, where this line of thinking takes me. And, although I don't want to go there, it is October 15, so of course I go there.

I arrive in Astorga in the late afternoon. It has been a week and a half since I've found myself in any place other than a small village that has the Camino, temporarily renamed Calle Mayor (Main Street), running through its tranquil center. Astorga is something else entirely. It is not just a stop along the Camino, it is a bustling tourist destination. It takes a while to reunite with Kiki, to find the albergue and settle in, to wash out socks and a shirt for tomorrow, to take a shower, to begin the mental transition from the quiet of the trail to the noise of this city.

It is a city made for wandering, not as glorious as León but still an eye-opener. Tom would have loved it here: the massive cathedrals, the expansive stone plazas, the city hall that looks like a basilica, a fanciful Museo del Chocolate (Astorga is reputed to be the European birthplace of chocolate), several lively commercial streets with dozens of shops selling branded Astorga chocolate, and then, the showstopper, a palace designed by Gaudí that looks like a hallucination. Tom would not have loved getting here—the predawn departure, the twenty-two-mile walk, the snacks that substitute for lunch. But he would have loved this moment: sitting on a bench in front of the Gaudí Palace in the warmth of a waning afternoon, eating a chocolate bar, and staring at this impossibility of a building with its mash-up of architectural influences, its columns and arches and flutes, its tower topped with a pinnacle that looks like a witch's hat. It is almost exhaustingly whimsical. We would have marveled at it, laughed at it, eaten more chocolate, wondered aloud what the Swiss would say about Astorga's claims to chocolate primacy. We would have walked the streets until we found a little restaurant, ordered paella, wandered some more, stayed in a lovely little Airbnb.

It occurs to me, imagining this scene, fantasizing about what today would be like if Tom were here, that my plan to flatten or temporarily forget the significance of this day is not working. It gets worse. I begin to replay the chronology of that day one year ago, the long walk down a country lane with the boys while Tom slept, Lizzie's arrival, the talks he managed to have with each of the children in between coughing fits. The medications sitting in the little box on the mantel. The way Jackson performed an energy-clearing ritual that Tom had taught him. When he asked, so quietly, for all of us to leave the room for a few minutes. *Stop it*, I tell myself. *This is maudlin and self-indulgent. This is how grief drowns you. This is how you participate in the drowning.* And so, I force myself to redirect my thoughts. Surely something else happened on that day one year ago. Suddenly, I want to know. I need to know that things happened that day that had nothing to do with us, that the world continued as if we were not there watching Tom die.

I sit on the bench, and I do the unpilgrim thing that I have seen so many others do: I take out my phone, connect to Wi-Fi, and sit there, hunched over, reading from the little screen. And I learn:

On this day, one year ago, the US recorded ninety thousand new COVID infections. Three suicide bombers attacked a Shiite mosque in Kandahar. A top administrator at a Texas school district told teachers they should present "opposing" perspectives to the Holocaust. Another woman accused Bill Cosby of drugging and raping her. Finally, deep into my scrolling—arrests, deadly fires, protests, rising rents, Dave Chappelle, Steve Bannon—I find an announcement that both the New York Cat Film Festival and the New York Dog Film Festival are returning to Manhattan after a pandemic-induced hiatus. This is a good place to stop.

It is a six-minute walk to the Plaza Mayor, the city's central square. I stroll slowly, thinking about what I will say to my sons when I call them in a few minutes. We've prearranged this time. I sit at a small table along the perimeter of the square and order a glass of vino tinto, talking first to Jackson, then Zane, the phone connection so crisp that it sounds as if six blocks, not six thousand miles, separate us. We don't talk about Tom. We talk about what's happening in their lives and how my journey is going. I describe the dawn and tell them I will send a photo. I entertain them with the story of James, the drunken, aging hippie with the way-too-young-for-him girlfriend. Kiki and I now refer to James as "the mayor of Fly Town." The story gets better every time I tell it. It could be any conversation—caring but lighthearted, engaged but not overly inquisitive, pleasant, mostly superficial. I just want to hear their voices. I think it's important that they hear mine. We do not talk about grief or death. None of us mentions the significance of this day.

Their grief is different from mine. They have his genes. I do not. They knew Tom their entire lives. I met him after high school and college, after moving back and forth across the country, after living in five different cities, after two serious boyfriends. I have a past that does not include him. They do not.

I think also about how their lives, their daily lives, have probably not changed that much since Tom's death. They are both happily partnered, employed, with hobbies and pastimes, with lives that have their own rhythms and soundtracks. At family dinners or brunches or holiday gatherings, Tom's absence is palpable. But otherwise? Every day? I wonder if they are as triggered as I am. I know I will not ask, I have not asked, because that, in itself, is a trigger.

I think also there is a significant difference in what I once read was called *anticipatory grief.* The children knew their father had a terminal illness, and they knew he was choosing to die on his own terms. But they knew this late in the game—Tom wanted it that way—and I knew it much earlier. I "anticipated" my grief as I watched Tom decline, as I listened to his cough, as I arranged our lives around his illness. They were, happily, not in the trenches with me, with Tom and me. Maybe that was a good buffer. Maybe it provided a less fraught space in which to come to terms with his impending death. Regardless, it was a different experience from what I had. They also have live-in, moment-to-moment emotional support if they need it. I can pay some stranger to listen to me. I can, ever so hesitantly, every once in a while, sit across from a friend and let them in on a sliver of my life. But I can't turn my head on the pillow at night and talk to the person who knows me as much as I have ever let anyone know me.

My sons have more future than past. I do not.

As I listen to their voices, and later, as I lie in a single bed next to Kiki's single bed in a private room we managed to score, I think, *This is your "anniversary" present, Tom. These boys, these men, your sons. They are tall, like you, with those long arms, "gorilla arms," you called them, that make the sleeves of off-the-rack shirts hit far above the wrist. They can grow great beards like yours. They are smart and funny like you. Quick-witted. Sometimes know-it-alls but charming about it. They learned other things from you about how to navigate manhood. They are extraordinary young men because they had a father like you. One is supposed to mark milestones, to celebrate anniversaries. This is something to celebrate.*

17

THEY ARE OUT IN the meadow in front of the house, my husband and my daughter. It is late fall. The trees are bare; the grass is blindingly green and slick from two months of rain. Tom is wearing the grimy, too-small-for-his-supersize-head fishing cap he picked up in Alaska on one of the trips with his father and the Gore-Tex jacket I bought him several birthdays ago. His beard is luxuriant but under control and has yet to show a touch of gray. Lizzie, age seven, is dressed in flowery purple leggings with matching sweatshirt. Her coat lies off to the side in the wet grass.

They are playing a made-up game, part tag, part red-light-green-light, part chase-the-deer-away. They stop after a while, breathing hard, and face each other. Tom reaches out to grab

Lizzie's hand. He lifts her, and she plants her wet, grubby sneakers, one by one, on his blue-jeaned thighs. His knees are bent slightly. He is leaning backward. She leans back the opposite way, mirroring his stance, both of their free arms flung out to the side. They are looking forward, beaming, holding the pose, a kind of acrobatic finale ta-da of this private performance. The stance is both precarious—any movement might unbalance them—yet absolutely solid. Of course, Tom would adjust. He would keep Lizzie aloft.

I watch from the porch. I take this picture. They don't notice me.

These glimpses I catch of them when they don't know I am looking? They say so much about who they are—not separately, not father and daughter, not father-playing-with-daughter, but the duo they create. I watch them one day the following spring walking the fence line. Lizzie is taller. Her hair is shorter. Her face is changing from little girl to young adolescent. It is a beautiful face. Tom is wearing his Alaska fishing cap and has that parental this-is-a-teaching-moment look on his face. He is holding a wildflower in his hands. It's a cat's-ear lily, small and delicate, with soft, hairy-edged petals that look like . . . cats' ears. He is bending down to talk to her. She is now perhaps half his height, her head mid-rib length to his body. His look is familiar, that professorial look I have seen so often, with her, with the boys, even with me. He is the most curious person I have ever met, perhaps the most curious person I will ever meet, and he loves nothing more than sharing what he has learned. When I jump on a teaching moment with Lizzie, I get the thousand-yard stare or, lately, the eye roll. Tom gets the look he is getting right now: wonderment. With a touch of adoration. Maybe more than a touch.

They had something, these two. They were easy with each other. I could see it in their body language. I could hear it in their voices. Lizzie loved Tom in that way daughters can love their fathers, deeply but without the prickly intensity that so often marks the relationship between daughters and mothers. Some studies report that daughters may feel less judged and more emotionally supported by fathers, particularly during adolescence. I don't know who all was studied, but I know Tom and Lizzie, and I know—I knew then, and I know now—that this is how she felt. Of course there was conflict, but where I leaned into it, Tom stepped back. He gave her room. I pushed, mostly (I thought) gently, for her to *do*—whatever the "do" was, whatever the "something" was. He didn't. Between Lizzie and me, there always seemed to be a sense of urgency. Between father and daughter, there was calm. Their love was soft and playful. It had a steadiness to it, unlike the roller coaster of our mother-daughter love. And it had a beautiful simplicity: She admired him. He accepted her.

There were other moments they shared, other experiences, some of which were so ordinary—or so it seemed to me at the time—that they hardly registered. Now I see how special they were. There were years living out in the country when we did not have garbage service. We had a compost bin out in the garden, but the garbage and the recycling had to be loaded in the back of the minivan and taken to the dump. Tom did this every other Saturday with Lizzie eagerly riding shotgun. I hated driving the minivan, a big, boxy gas hog that was a necessity with three kids, and I hated going to the dump. But the two of them looked forward to it. I thought nothing more of it than that: a chore I didn't have to do or be involved with in any way. Now I conjure an image of them out there, with Tom schooling Lizzie about recycling, the two of them going bin to bin with our jars and cans and newspapers. And I see them out there making this objectively unpleasant, skunky experience into a game: *Can you name all the terrible smells you're smelling? Let's make retching noises together*. Did they do this? I don't know. But something happened out there that made them return with smiles (and clothes that needed to be shed immediately in the mudroom and washed in hot water). I later discovered—it was one of my sons who let me in on the secret—that they routinely stopped at IHOP on the way home and ate their way through the Rooty Tooty Fresh 'N Fruity breakfast bonanza. Maybe that accounted for the smiles.

During those years, he taught her how to operate the riding mower. I was not a fan of this activity, which I considered both borderline dangerous and premature. The meadow that needed mowing was uneven, with outcroppings of rocks you sometimes didn't see until it was almost too late. And Lizzie was still several birthdays away from learning how to drive a car. But she had sat on Tom's lap for years as he operated the machine. He let her hold the steering wheel. She placed her hand on top of his when he engaged the gearshift. On the flattest stretch, he let her steer. Then, one sunny afternoon when she was maybe thirteen or fourteen, he starts up the mower, dismounts and lets her go by herself. Her legs are long enough now that she can reach the gas pedal. She grabs the steering wheel with one hand, engages the gear with the other, and off she goes. Tom trots alongside, just as I had done years before when I released my grip on the seat of her two-wheeler and let her ride her bike for the first time by herself. After that, the meadow mowing became her chore, one she looked forward to, unlike the others—putting her laundry away, clearing the dishes—that she grumbled about. I think I was the one who taught her how to drive, practicing in the high school parking lot on Sundays. But really, she already knew.

Tom started a tradition of taking the kids, one at a time, on a special trip, just with him, when they were twelve. He took Jackson to Washington, DC, and they geeked out together at the Smithsonian, the National Air and Space Museum, National Museum of Natural History, and, believe it or not, the National Postal Museum. They returned sated with information, which together and separately they shared until they saw our eyes glaze over. Actually, I think they just kept sharing.

Two years later, when it was Zane's turn, the trip was somewhat less successful. Tom had to drag an unusually sullen Zane to the museums. All he wanted to do was stay in the hotel room and watch cartoons, an activity not common (as in: not allowed) in his everyday life. Zane was a happy, even-tempered kid, a get-along-with-everyone middle child, so his attitude was a mystery. Tom assessed the situation, told me about it in a lengthy phone call, and then took it in stride. He had the ability to ride those waves. They found a restaurant with giant burgers. They went to an old-fashioned barbershop. He transformed the trip on the fly.

When it was Lizzie's turn several years later, he didn't have another DC trip in him, and she was spectacularly uninterested in anything that appeared to be educational on what was supposed to be a vacation. Given that, I am not sure how he sold the Muscle Shoals, Alabama–Knoxville, Tennessee, trip they took together. It was part of the research he was doing for one of his books, so it was obviously educational, but I bet the big appeal for Lizzie was: *I get Dad all to myself. And I get to see Dad work.* She knew he was a writer, of course. But the part of his writing life she knew about was him disappearing into his office and staring at a screen. Now she could see him in action. It's hard to imagine she was thrilled touring power plants and corporate headquarters, but she *was* thrilled being treated like an adult. Lizzie struggled making and keeping friends her own age, but she was always good with older people, preternaturally poised, a charmer. She charmed all of Tom's sources. For years later, one man in particular, an avuncular Southern gentleman with a daughter a few years younger than Lizzie, sent her a box of treats from the Deep South for Christmas, along with a handwritten note about his delight in meeting her.

We took many trips as a family, modest ones mostly, by car: to the coast, over the mountains to the sunny part of Oregon, to a high-desert horse ranch, down to San Francisco. Our farthest-flung adventures were to Disney World, where we stayed in a resort that played Jimmy Buffett songs all day on the PA; and later, to Mexico, where one day Lizzie, then in the early years of high school, disappeared for hours. We had half the staff of the hotel looking for her and had called the police. Late in the afternoon, while Tom and I were on the beach getting another "no sighting" report from the policía, Lizzie came sauntering toward us, smiling, holding a plastic sack with several whole fish. While the rest of us were playing in the surf, she had befriended a grandfatherly fisherman who'd invited her to go out on the bay with him. One can imagine at least two horrible scenarios, neither of which had anything to do with this sweet old man and the lovely time they had on his boat. This was the quintessential Lizzie: a risk-taker who didn't even realize she was taking a risk. And this was the quintessential Tom: He took her aside and calmly, quietly, explained how she needed to check in with us before she went off on adventures. Then he praised her fishing ability, and together, they walked back to the old fisherman and insisted he accept payment for the fish. And where was I? Sobbing in relief while fuming at my daughter. At dinner, we were presented with a platter of grilled snapper, grouper, and sea bass. The hotel had cleaned and cooked the fish for us.

On this same trip, a few days later, Tom and Lizzie go off together. They have tickets to one of those touristy excursions—a boat ride to a protected area to swim with sea lions. It seems a little cheesy to me and the boys, not to mention expensive, but Lizzie wants to do it. And really, so does Tom. Parenthood gives you that kind of excuse, should you need it, to do those things you wouldn't do otherwise, like take a hayride through a pumpkin patch or try out every wooden horse on a vintage carousel or go to an indoor trampoline gym, all of which we did, as a family. But in Mexico, the two of them had this day to themselves. What I know about it is this: In Tom's office, on top of one of his bookcases, sat a framed photo, an image taken by the excursion photographer. The photographer caught the moment when Lizzie emerged from the water, her hair slicked back, an impossibly wide grin on her face. She is not a little girl anymore, not even an adolescent. She is in her teens. She has overtweezed her eyebrows, double-pierced her ears, and changed the color of her hair multiple times, each iteration—red, gold, copper, highlights, lowlights, streaked, hennaed—as pretty as the next. In this photo, her hair is every color at once: wheat, honey, caramel, russet. The sea lion's head, almost twice the size of hers, is half out of the water, and so close to hers that they are almost touching. The sea lion's mouth is open wide. This animal could bite off Lizzie's head in one chomp. She is unaware, frozen in a moment of exuberance. This image is all about that sense of innocence and emotional freedom when you can't imagine that anything will ever go wrong. And it is about fearlessness. Lizzie was, for better and worse, fearless. Or wanted to be. Or pretended to be. I don't know. I am looking at this picture now. I moved it into my office. It is on my bookcase. What I see is my daughter thunderstruck by joy.

18

CLOSELY FOLLOWING THE *I'm so sorry I will never do it again* script used by those who commit acts of domestic violence, Lizzie's boyfriend, FA, now released from his shockingly short ninety-day stint behind bars for his violence against my child, bombards Lizzie with "give me another chance" texts. I know this because she shows them to me, scrolling through on her phone, reading aloud. She believes him, and she wants me to believe him too. FA tells her that he is "getting help," that he is "getting better." I ask her what kind of help he is getting. She doesn't know. Does he, has he ever, talked about therapy or support groups or medication? It is astonishing to me that his release from jail did not come with a mandate to participate in an anger management or domestic violence group. I know it came with probation restrictions. Isn't contacting Lizzie one of them? My quizzing feels like interrogation to her, I know that, but sometimes, at odd and wonderful times, she opens up to me, and I am hoping this will be one of those times. It isn't.

She is back living at our house, working four long graveyard shifts at the bakery, getting so good at what she does that the owner—who had come close to firing her—tells her one morning, after sampling her bakes, that she makes better bialys than he does. This is a very big deal, as he is stingy with praise and particularly proud of his own abilities. Lizzie is back to talking about plans to start her own little bakery, at first selling from a food truck or maybe a booth at the outdoor crafts-and-food market in town. For a week or so, Tom, Lizzie, and I engage in spirited talk and brainstorming. Lizzie and I experiment with recipes for malted milk ball cookies and almond dried cherry scones. And then, flip of a switch, she is withdrawn and weary, spending her off-hours either sleeping upstairs or on other people's couches. And then one morning, she returns from work to tell us that she's been fired. Only a few weeks ago, her boss heaped praise on her. She tells us what happened. For all her silences and secrets, her stonewalling and eye-rolling, she can be startlingly forthcoming.

FA started showing up at her work again, she tells us. She works alone in a small kitchen that is a few doors down from the bakery storefront. She let him in the first few times, and it was good, she said. Tom and I exchange a look. My look says: *I cannot believe this is happening.* His look says to me: *Shut up and listen. She is actually talking to us.* The next time he came by at three or four in the morning, he stayed through most of her shift, blasting metal music and distracting her from working. Then he pushed her against the dough machine. The next time he came by, she didn't unlock the door. He banged on it until she did. Inside, there was pushing and shoving that ended with an accident. Two hotel sheet pans with bagels ready for the oven crashed to the floor. The cleanup took a while. Remaking two dozen bagels—mixing, kneading, proofing, boiling, and baking—took so long that several batches of muffins didn't get made in time for the opening of the bakery. The owner was not happy. She didn't explain what had happened. She took the blame.

A few nights later, he came by again. Again, she did not open the door. Again, he banged. It is unclear—either Lizzie doesn't know or she isn't telling—how the owner got wind of this. But he did. There was something else going on there in the wee hours, including an increasing number of "visits" from other sketchy acquaintances looking for fresh-baked handouts and, Lizzie much later told us, a break-in of her car. This was a lot. The owner didn't need that kind of drama happening at his business, with the potential of, as he undoubtedly and correctly saw it, personal injury or property damage. He fired her. I wasn't angry at him. He was protecting his business. I wasn't even, at that time, angry at FA. Whether he had diagnosed (or undiagnosed) mental illness or was just a deplorable lout, he was who he was. He had shown himself for who he was. I was angry at Lizzie, Lizzie the mighty discus thrower, the only girl on her middle school's wrestling team, the daughter of a card-carrying feminist, the daughter of a man who modeled kindness and respect. *How could she!* I failed to see then, or rather failed to appreciate, the enormous stress of the life she was leading, regardless of how much of that was her choice.

It is hard to write about Lizzie, about her life, about her descent into addiction, about how it all ended. Well-brought-up middle-class children, with the advantages of a stable home and a loving family, are not supposed to become drug addicts. Parents are supposed to protect their children from harm. Children are not supposed to die before their parents. The pain of writing about this—which is the pain of thinking about it, reliving it, excavating it—is not just, or mostly, about the facts of it. It is about the guilt of it. What didn't we see? What should we have seen? What didn't we do? What should we have done? How could I, how could we, have prevented this from happening? What kind of a mother am I?

With Tom, there were some regrets. Yes, we should have talked more about the state of our marriage as we moved through the decades. Yes, we could have done better. But we were mostly kind. We were loyal and dependable partners. And especially during the last year of his life, I was there. I was there in all the ways he wanted me to be there and needed me to be there. I did the big things and the little things. I shouldered as much of the burden as I could, which was a lot. With Tom, with thinking about and relating his part of the story, I have a sense of peace that parallels the sorrow. With Lizzie, there is a heavy overlay of guilt, even though I know, with a person in the maw of addiction, you cannot *make* them stop. And shame. Because isn't it always the mother's fault?

As I deconstruct this period in her life, I wonder how well I actually knew her. How much did she let me know her? I think of all I kept to myself as a child, an adolescent, a teen growing up. I don't mean secret cigarette smoking or taking an occasional swig from the vodka bottle in the liquor cabinet; I mean who I was, what I felt, what I wanted. I behaved. I checked the boxes that needed to be checked. But what thoughts I had, what emotions I felt, what coming-of-age angst I felt I suffered, the Sturm und Drang of my unremarkable suburban life? I wrote about this in a locked diary I kept between the mattress and the box spring of my bed. I never, ever, had a soul-searching conversation with my mother. I left home the moment I could.

Lizzie was more complicated. Sometimes it seemed to me that she overshared. But then I was always conscious of what she chose to overshare. Sometimes it seemed to me that she was the child I was closest to: the Wednesday afternoons during elementary school that we spent together at pet stores or tea shops or at home baking and attempting craft projects; the adventures we shared hiking in Utah; when we saw the traveling show of *Wicked* and spent the next six months blasting "Defying Gravity" in the car; the time we each got *XO* tattooed on the insides of our right wrists. And other times, she was the child I didn't understand at all.

After she was fired, after FA showed yet again who he really was, after she could no longer avoid facing the fact that, regardless of what he said or promised, regardless of declarations of love, he was not about to change, Lizzie's life changed. She stayed in her room, sleeping most of the day. This didn't seem odd, because she had become accustomed to upside-down hours. But at night, when she would have been working or hanging out at the dive bar or camping out on friends' couches, she didn't leave the house. She didn't want to go anywhere, see anyone, do anything. Or talk to us. I think she was scared of physical harm, but that was only part of it. I also think she was coming to realize the emotional and psychological wounds she had suffered and would continue to suffer if this man stayed in her life. I hated that she was scared, this bold girl of mine with her wide streak of fearlessness. But both Tom and I were elated that she seemed ready to extricate herself from this dangerous and toxic relationship. She didn't say anything, but she didn't have to. She was ready for a change. And we were ready with a plan.

We offered Lizzie the little house on the coast, the one Tom and I had bought a decade before and used as both a writing retreat and a family vacation getaway. She could live out there, far from FA and the life she had been leading. She could recover—it was that kind of place—and then start fresh, find a job, make friends. We would visit from time to time, but the place would be hers. She had never had a place of her own. When we sat down to talk about this, to work out details, it was the first time I had seen Lizzie smile in a very long time.

She was serious about a fresh start. She got off social media, changed her phone number, blocked FA, told no one where she was going. This she did, all of it, on her own initiative. One afternoon, while she was upstairs in her room packing up her clothes, I placed my Bluetooth speaker on the floor next to her closed door and blasted Tom Petty's "Into the Great Wide Open." She came out, grinning, and we sang it together, loudly: "The future was wide open."

And she was off.

In short order, she found a job. The town was small, but summer vacationers and second-home owners helped support several decent restaurants, including an iconic breakfast spot. Her job, the lowliest of the low, was to come in after closing and clean the place. The hip new owners loved her. She was quickly promoted to the kitchen, first assisting with food prep, then managing the grill station, then taking over as what a fancier place would have called a sous chef. She was also given the responsibility of shopping for the restaurant based on the next week's menu. She was learning about the business. She was gaining confidence. She was making fifty cents over minimum wage. This worked because we were footing almost all her living expenses: housing, utilities, insurance, phone. It was a time of transition. We were helping her get on her feet. Meanwhile, we texted back and forth but otherwise stayed out of her new life. We didn't go out to the beach house. This was tough for me. I had spent a lot of time out there, often by myself. I had written most of two books sitting at a desk I cobbled together from some old furniture and stuck in a corner nook in the upstairs loft. Our family of five had squeezed into the space, sleeping on couches and floors and had the kind of simple adventures families have when nothing is planned, and the sun is shining, and you're at the beach.

After several months of cheerful, newsy texts, the tone of her messages changed. She criticized the owner, found fault with the way things were being handled, didn't like several of her coworkers. The head cook was mean to her. She was given responsibility for lunch service and was nervous and overwhelmed. And then, suddenly, there was a text announcing the news of a new job, this one at a local watering hole, a dive bar out on the highway. Whether she left the restaurant or was fired, she didn't say. At the new place, she was hired as a barback—stocking liquor, polishing glasses, refilling garnishes—with aspirations to tend bar. There were enthusiastic texts about the people she worked with, about how much she was learning, about the great tips, about how much she loved the job. Until she didn't. Or they cut back on her shifts. Or something. The job lasted two months. After that, there was a kitchen position at a very good restaurant, then a baking job, then a food cart job, each one greeted with excitement, each one short-lived.

I am appalled now thinking about how it did not occur to us that some if not all of what was happening might be drug related. We knew that FA was a user. Lizzie told us this. He had a history with heroin, and he smoked and snorted meth. She also told us that she did not, that she knew the dangers, that she was helping him taper off. We wanted to believe her. After all, this is what she did: She found broken people and tried to fix them. And we put trust in her upbringing, trust—I later realized, so misplaced—in the notion that good kids from good backgrounds didn't make terrible decisions. Did she first encounter methamphetamine in FA's shack? Did the temporary euphoria or spark of energy he got from meth appeal to her? Did her topsy-turvy work-sleep schedule, her hours and hours of standing on her feet operating industrial mixers, hefting pans, moving quickly from task to task, did this open the door to the use of stimulants? I don't know. And I don't know whether, if I had known back then, it would have made a difference. She told us what she wanted to tell us. She told us what she knew we wanted to hear. Maybe she started using meth before FA. I would like to blame him. Every parent wants to blame someone else for the downfall of their child.

Now, safely away from FA, on her own, she might have been using drugs to quiet her anxieties, to blunt the trauma of what she had been through, to quell loneliness, to increase wakefulness, to give her energy for work, to decrease appetite, for many reasons, and then maybe, over time, for only one reason: because she was becoming addicted. I knew so little. I understood so little. Back then, I thought, in my generous moments, *Okay, this is going to take some time. This is a tough transition. She just hasn't found the right job yet. The path of life is rocky. She has the skills to navigate it. We taught and modeled those skills.* And in my judgmental moments, I thought, *What the hell? Why doesn't she get her act together?*

Six months after she moves to the beach house, I get a text from Lizzie. Things have been quiet for a little while. She has told us that she loves the new job at the food cart. The owners have had her over for dinner. She works daylight hours. The tips are good. I try not to get too excited. There have been so many ups and downs. But still, when she is happy, I am happy. Tom and I are at a get-together in another coastal town about two hours away from the beach house. We're sitting around a driftwood fire drinking Oregon pinot when my phone vibrates. I pull it out of my pocket and read this: *FA here pounding the door.* I am cold and hot at the same time. I pull Tom aside and show him the text. FA? How does he know where she lives? How has he found her? We call the local police—the town has three officers—give them the address of the beach house and rush out to our car. It will take two hours to get there, and two hours is a very long time. Just a few minutes into the drive, I get a call from one of the local cops. He drove out to the house—it's maybe a minute from the police station—and reports that no one was there. I ask him if there was a car in front. He says no. I tell him that Lizzie owns a car. I describe it. Tom remembers part of the license plate number. The cop puts in a call to the state police with an alert for the car.

This feels like it is happening to someone else.

Tom and I are quiet in the car, stunned, spinning our separate scenarios that we don't want to share. He is driving much faster than he should on this serpentine, two-lane road that skirts the cliffs along the ocean. When we are about a half hour away, I get another call from the local officer. He has been so attentive, so focused, his voice so measured. And kind. He tells us that the state police sighted Lizzie's car on the highway—the same highway we're traveling, maybe fifty miles to the north of us—and pulled it over. Lizzie was driving. A man was in the passenger seat. He is identified as FA. The state cop asked Lizzie to get out of the car so he could talk to her privately, away from FA. Meanwhile, his partner runs FA's name through whatever databases the police have to check on people. His name doesn't show up.

When the local cop tells me this on the phone, I am speechless. How can this be? FA was sentenced to jail for domestic violence crimes, and part of that sentence, after jail time, was thirty-six months of probation. The document from the circuit court couldn't have been more definite: "The Defendant is . . . prohibited from knowingly going within sight of [my daughter] and from going to her residence, place of employment, or school." He has clearly violated the terms of probation. When I find my voice again, I tell this all to the cop. *Why didn't his name show up?* I ask the cop. *Why didn't the state police take him into custody right then?* He doesn't know. But, because his name was not in the database, and because Lizzie—undoubtedly terrified—told the officer she was "okay," they had to let them go.

Where, we do not know.

19

I KNOW RAIN. I have lived in western Oregon for most of my adult life, where it can—and has—rain as much as twenty inches in a single month. During my first winter in Oregon, it rained for seventy-nine days. Every day for seventy-nine days. I *know* rain. And I love rain. I love falling asleep under a down comforter in the dead of winter with the windows thrown open to the hiss of rain. I love awakening to the soft aqueous light that is a painter's dream and listening to the rush of water in the culvert. I love the thrum of rain against the house on a dark afternoon, the peaceful tedium of long, wet days. I love the fine mist on my face, the way my skin feels soft and pliant and new in the rain.

This is what I tell myself as Kiki and I set off in the sheeting rain from the picturesque ancient village of Rabanal where we had spent the night. In the small, dark, stone-walled restaurant attached to the small, dark, stone-walled accommodations we found, my companion finally got to order *cocido maragato*, a dish she'd been talking about for days. She'd thoroughly researched this iconic "reverse stew," made notations in her Moleskine notebook about it, and was, in her words, "hell-bent" on finding it. It arrived at our table in a trough with blood sausage, chorizo, pig's trotters, pig's ear, pork ribs, hunks of fat, and chunks of bone, all floating in a cabbagey, garbanzo-y soup. You eat the meat first, then the vegetables, then the soup, thus the "reverse stew" idea. I had to leave the table twice to avoid watching her eat. Now, walking a few paces in front of her as we trudge up an elevation gain of twelve hundred feet, I wonder—but do not want to ask—how all those pork products are sitting in her gut.

We are headed up to the high point on the Camino Francés, the Cruz de Ferro, the Iron Cross. The ascent, which will take us to five thousand feet, is alternately rocky and muddy, slippery, challenging, and as little fun as I've had in a while. The rain is unrelenting, occasionally approaching deluge, every once in a while coming in at a slant, momentarily blinding. I am wearing the cheap plastic poncho I bought a week or two ago, which covers my backpack and me, but plastic doesn't breathe. So, I am just as wet under the poncho from the sweat of the uphill hike as I would be without the poncho.

I have lost my affection for rain.

I have also lost my sense of humor.

I am particularly annoyed with Kiki, not because of that gruesome dinner but because I sometimes see in her the qualities

I least like in myself. One in particular: She refuses help. Earlier that morning, as we see the heavy-bellied, blue-black clouds cross the sky and begin to feel the first spits of rain, I watch as Kiki struggles to reach around to the side pocket of her backpack to grab her poncho. We are standing off to the side of the path, a few kilometers out of Rabanal. I've already put on my poncho, adjusted my Idaho Potato Museum ball cap under the hood, and readied myself for what is sure to come. Kiki is trying to grab her gear.

"Let me help you," I say. She takes a small step back from me so I can't reach her pack. "No," she says. "I can do it myself." It's the way she says it, not the words. Her tone tells me she has taken offense. I watch her twist her torso, torquing it hard to the right. Her hand fishes around until it manages to grab hold of a corner of the poncho, which is stuffed down deep in the pocket. With effort, she extricates it. *I can do it myself.* I watch and think, *Yes, I know you can do it yourself. That's not why I am offering.* And in that moment, I see myself so clearly it just about floors me.

Kiki is my mirror. I am the one who almost always refuses help. I am the one—like Kiki—who conflates being helped with being helpless, who interprets an offer of assistance as a criticism of my abilities. "I can do it myself" had pretty much been my motto for as long as I could remember. I can do it myself, I said during my cancer treatment. I can do it myself, I said in that year between Tom's diagnosis and death. I can do it myself, I said when faced with my daughter's death. Sometimes it takes someone else doing just what you have done, saying just what you would have said, to shake you awake. It occurs to me, there in the incipient downpour, in the mud, at the beginning of a day that promises to be tough, watching my companion struggle (successfully, *of course*) to extract the poncho, that when someone offers help, it may have absolutely nothing to do with whether they think you're capable of handling the situation by yourself. I knew Kiki was capable. I had seen her grab the poncho a dozen times or more. I offered my help to be of service, to perform a small act of kindness, to show friendship, to connect in the moment. When Kiki refused (as I had so many times refused such offers, as I had, in fact, gone out of my way to not encounter such offers), she was not just proclaiming her self-sufficiency, she was depriving me of this opportunity to be a friend. Of course, she didn't do it for that reason, or knowingly, just as I had not all those many times I had refused such offers. In doing so, had I rebuffed friendship? Erected barriers? Hurt those who wanted to help? Created distance?

I think about this, but I stop myself before I slide into regret and recrimination. This is history. I can't do anything about the past. But I can, maybe, take to heart—a cliché, I know, but an apt one—this important lesson the Camino, and Kiki, are trying to teach me: *Accepting help* and *being helpless* are not the same. Whether I will learn this after a lifetime of acting differently, I don't know. But I intend to try. I also realize that there is an even harder lesson embedded in this one: It is not just about learning how to *receive* help with grace. It is about being able to *ask* for help. I have told myself, and I have come to believe, that asking for help means you are incapable of handling it yourself. It is an announcement of your own weakness. You know: *I've fallen, and I can't get up.*

Today, right now, I do need help. I have needed help since that evening in the "truck stop albergue" three days ago when I got the email from the state medical examiner's office, the email with the attachment, the attachment that was the autopsy report, the report that listed the substances found in my daughter's blood. The help I needed was simple, really. I just needed to tell someone. The help was in the telling. "All sorrows can be borne if you put them into a story or tell a story about them," Karen Blixen once wrote. And yes, I know, that is just what I am doing right now. But then the wound was so fresh, still bleeding. It seemed, then, unstaunchable. I considered, for the briefest of moments, reaching out to my sons. But I could not, I would not, be responsible for adding to their burdens. They had lost a father. They had lost a sister. What they needed, I told myself, was an invincible mother. I would be that. I would pretend to be that. But there was someone else I could tell, the someone who was sitting across the dinner table from me when the email came through on my phone, who was sleeping in a narrow cot next to mine when, that night, I opened the attachment and read the report, the someone who was now walking beside me in the rain.

That, however, was asking for help. It was burdening someone with my sorrow. It was presenting them with a situation that could not be changed, could not be made better, and for which there was no adequate response. I thought about the whispery-voiced *I'm so sorry for your loss* responses I had gotten when Tom had died. I could not bear that again. And I did not want it from Kiki, who respected me for the strength she thought I had. Better not to show weakness. Or what I then perceived as showing weakness.

Instead, I pulled down the visor of the ball cap, cinched the hood of the poncho tight around my face, walked in rain and in silence, and thought about the report. Maybe because *autopsy* is a creepy word, it was called *Forensic Examination Report*. My daughter, my Lizzie, was the "decedent," with "the body of a well-developed white woman" with "all body organs in their normal, anatomical positions." It was noted that she had a tattoo of the sun on her back—she had gotten this the day after her high school graduation—and on "the anterior aspect of the right forearm"—her wrist—there was "black inscription 'XO.'"

The cause of death was "acute fentanyl and methamphetamine toxicity." In other words, an overdose. I would not find out until months later, when I was able to talk with a toxicologist, an ER physician, and a drug counselor, what this meant, exactly, how it wasn't the meth that killed her but rather the fentanyl that had been added, only a small amount, a very small amount. But enough. And it wasn't actually the drugs that killed her; neither was it the massive swelling in her brain—"severe cerebral edema" in the words of the report—that the drugs caused. Yes, the swelling increased the pressure inside her brain, which compressed the blood vessels, which impeded the flow of blood and oxygen to the brain. Her brain starved. But, as my ER doc friend later explained, in clinical, dispassionate detail, even before that, even before her brain swelled, the drug interfered with messages to her brain to breathe. She asphyxiated.

This is a lot to think about while trudging up a muddy path in the rain. It is a lot to hold inside.

In the late morning, in the steady rain, in silence, Kiki and I make the final ascent leading to the Cruz de Ferro. I am expecting something inspiring of awe. Kiki had told me earlier that this spot was a significant landmark with deep meaning for pilgrims. It was, she said, one of the most iconic and emotionally charged markers on the five-hundred-mile trek. It signified both a literal and figurative peak for pilgrims, a place of deep contemplation and prayer, a symbol of faith and humility. I am now accustomed to the fact that Kiki seems to know everything about this route. This is sometimes wonderful, like having access to a walking, talking Wikipedia entry. And it is sometimes too much. I like not knowing. I like testing my ability to welcome surprise, to accept what I encounter along the way. This is why I purposely under-researched this trip. The recent surprises in my life have not been good ones. But there are good ones out there. I need to remember that. In fact, Kiki is one of those surprises, so mostly I listen with interest.

The origins of this special place are unclear, Kiki had told me, but it is believed that the site dates back to Roman times with the placing of a stone cairn on this high point. It might be that an abbot from a nearby monastery erected an earlier version of the cross in the eleventh century as a guidepost for medieval pilgrims. This is not exactly a sacred place, she told me, but it comes close.

What I see in front of me, as I tip my head up from under the hood of the poncho, has none of the splendor and gravitas I was anticipating. It is just a very tall pole with a simple metal cross mounted on top. It is modest—except for its sixteen-foot height—unadorned, artless, inelegant. Sitting atop a very large mound of stones, it looks almost ugly. But I find its plainness appealing. Walking through the small villages along the way, many of them underpopulated, some of them with neglected, crumbling, boarded-up stone buildings, I had been struck by the contrast of the refinement of the often tiny churches in those same struggling villages. Even the humblest of those churches had a touch of, to my eyes, out-of-place wealth: a stained glass window, a decorative altar, an ornate crucifix. It was hard not to think about the poverty of the villagers and the wealth of the Catholic Church, of the sacrifices made to keep the little churches in so much better repair than many of the buildings. But here at the Cruz de Ferro, there is no elegance, no wealth, just a very tall pole planted on a pile of rocks situated at the highest elevation on this pilgrimage. There is a purity to that.

Kiki, who is not only a walking encyclopedia but is also a knowledgeable if semilapsed Catholic, had told me, as we were walking that morning, that pilgrims create a personal ceremony at the cross, leaving a stone or trinket, some kind of memento, at the cross. It is something they've brought from home and carried with them to this high point on the path. The item, whatever it is, represents the struggles and burdens a person has carried with them, the literal weight of past worries. The act of carrying it and then leaving it behind symbolizes the shedding of this burden, a spiritual cleansing, perhaps even, for the believer, absolution.

I knew nothing of the cross itself as a marker on the journey, and I knew nothing about its significance. When I was packing back home, I had placed three small items to accompany me on the walk: the chakra worry stone I had left with Federico, the Oasis albergue hospitalero; a small stone of Tom's that he had been given by a Q'ero shaman in Peru; and Lizzie's metal cuff bracelet stamped with her name. The chakra stone was for me. The other items were just a way for me to feel like Tom and Lizzie were along on the journey. But there I was, at the Cruz de Ferro, with these two items I had carried on my back for more than two hundred miles. And here in front of me was this hallowed spot where thousands of pilgrims had placed commemorative items they had carried with them, believing that, in adding them to the pile, they were relinquishing their worries or troubles to a higher power.

There have been times I wished I believed in God, and this is one of them.

The rain is coming in sideways. The wind is whipping my plastic poncho, making sails of the sides. I would like to keep walking, to head down to the next village, wherever it is, get out of the weather, and sit quietly with a café con leche. But I know I must stop here. This was not part of a plan, but I decide to leave Tom's stone and Lizzie's bracelet on the mound. I off-load the backpack, find the stone and the bracelet in a little pocket, and climb up the massive pile of rocks that lead to the cross. It is slippery. I must watch where I'm stepping. I can see now that among the rocks and stones are beads and flags, ribbons, photos, poems and letters and prayers on slips of paper. There is a small stuffed teddy bear. There is a lock of hair. So many bits and pieces of so many lives. I don't think I fully appreciated until this moment that, although I have approached the Camino as a solitary expedition, an experience uniquely my own, I am in fact part of a collective journey. Of course, I know there are and have been for centuries others who walked this path. But it is seeing this heap of mementos, this pile of pain and longing and worry and troubles that people have tried to leave behind, that has given me a sense of community.

I find a place for Tom's stone and set Lizzie's bracelet on top of it. I think I'm supposed to say a prayer. But I don't pray. Instead, I tell my husband and my daughter, out loud, that I am leaving a bit of them here in Spain, that I think they will like it here, and that I love them. Of course, I am crying. The rest of that day, as I walk down, down, down along narrow winding paths, the sky as changeable as my mood—dark and foreboding, clearing and bright, then thick with rain clouds once again—I think: Did I leave anything behind when I left those items on the mound by the cross? Did I leave behind pain, grief? Guilt? Anger? Where's the catharsis?

Early that evening, having found a place to sleep, having exchanged my hiking shoes for flip-flops and washed out a pair of socks and a shirt for tomorrow, I am in a tienda looking to buy snacks for the trail. I stand in front of the produce bin eyeing the selection. Spain is famous for its oranges, and rightly so. I grab the two smallest, one in each hand, and try to assess their weights. I choose the one that feels the lightest. I do not need to be carrying any more than I already carry.

Midmorning the next day, I take the small orange from my pack and eat it sitting on a rock by the side of the path. When I heft the backpack on my shoulders again and position the straps, it feels lighter. Can it be that I can sense a four-ounce difference? I sit down again to think about this. I think about how the removal of one small item changed what I felt. I think about all these little things, and not-so-little things, in our lives, and how they add up. We stuff them in our metaphoric backpacks because we don't have time to deal with them or we don't want to deal with them or we don't know how to deal with them or we think we don't need to deal with them. And then, boom, the weight. The crushing weight. How do you get out from under that weight?

This being the Camino, Land of the Aha Moments, I have one: You don't have to process everything at once. You don't have to understand everything that has happened. You don't have to heal every wound. You can just lighten the load one four-ounce orange at a time.

20

WIDOW. WINDOW.

I am not trying to be clever. I am saying that widowhood is a window. Looking through it, you can view, assess, learn from, cry over, laugh about, regret, celebrate—everything—the marriage that was, the relationship that helped define you for decades. Falling in love is easy. A long marriage is hard. In its midst, you just live it, the peaks and the valleys, the days when you look over at him and think, *What an extraordinary human I am bound to*, and the other days when just listening to him chew makes you want to scream. There are years (the early ones) and times (waking up in a tent at dawn, walking the backstreets of Lucca, digging in the dirt to make a garden) when you feel you are living a life of enchantment. And then there are years, and times, when your married life feels like a hard climb in bad weather. I sound here as if I am delivering a lecture. I am. To myself.

When I first became a widow, I did not look through that window at my marriage. I could not bring myself to do that. I protected myself against the full force of grief by—I now realize—adopting two very different, even contradictory, mindsets. The first, and kindest, was contemplating the way Tom chose to end his life, the dignity and grace of that, the gift it was to the children and to me. I never admired him more than I did the day he died. I was, in fact, in awe. The awe was a shield against the pain I was not ready to feel.

My second approach, alas, was the opposite: I focused on the *hard climb in bad weather* parts of the marriage, the distance that had grown between us, the silences at the dinner table, the way we stopped dedicating our books to each other, the times I cried alone in the car. This allowed me to say to myself, *See, it wasn't that good after all. Not much to miss here. Move on.* This shield—or maybe it was a lens through which I was just beginning to sneak peeks through that window of widowhood—did its job. I may have seemed absurdly resilient to those around me, or I may have seemed cold and unfeeling. Neither was true. I was just armored, a useful and a terrible skill I had learned after our joint and simultaneous brush with mortality decades before.

Also, even absent my purposeful girding of the loins, I was, I am, a human with the evolutionary development of my species, which includes a well-researched psychological tendency called *negativity bias*. This means we often remember negative experiences more vividly and for longer periods than positive ones. I cannot explain the neurobiology of it, but I know it's a thing.

And I understand it evolved as a survival mechanism to help our cave-dwelling ancestors remember and avoid danger. How ironic. It helped me avoid the dangers of depression and anxiety and self-pity and generalized wallowing. Not exactly lions and tigers and bears.

I have since read that the frequency with which we reflect on memories strengthens those memories. It seems that when our thoughts travel those neural pathways so often, the pathways become paved and smooth, providing an easy trip down memory lane. That makes sense. This is just what I was doing during that first year, maybe more, after Tom died as I ruminated on all that I perceived had been missing from our marriage. But there is also this other human tendency, *positivity bias*, that is triggered by upbeat recollections, by telling the stories, to ourselves, to others, of happier times. I thought if I did this—looked at old photos, read the letters he sent to me when we lived a continent apart in the early days, reminisced with his sisters or my children—it would make me unbearably sad. I didn't think I could function under the weight of all those happy memories. But how, exactly, was I living under the weight of all that negativity? It looked good from the outside. How strong I was. How I was moving along, moving *on*, taking care of business. How I hadn't missed a beat. On the inside, it felt hollow, like I was a big, empty cavern.

Yesterday, cleaning my office, down on my hands and knees, I found a thumb drive wedged between two baskets under my desk. I had lost it so long ago that it didn't even look familiar. When I opened it up on my computer, I saw a PDF of a book I had been reading when I researched a biography I decided not to write, and a file of photos from a 2017 trip to Crete, and something named “annimov,” an MP4 file. I was clueless. I opened it, and for the next two minutes and thirty-four seconds, I listened to Van Morrison sing “Crazy Love” while watching a montage of photos Tom had curated that told the story, a story, of our life together. This “annimov” was an anniversary present Tom had given me in 2019, before the pandemic, before the diagnosis, before Lizzie’s descent, in ancient times.

I watched: Christmases in the living room, both of us in red nightshirts; me leaning against a stone wall in the Garfangnana; me in the kitchen carving a turkey; us in Renoir’s garden; hikes, so many hikes, rivers, mountains, glaciers. Who took that picture of us, so very young, kissing on the banks of the Deschutes? Or posed in front of that spidery backwoods cabin where we spent our honeymoon? I am seated in a lawn chair, writing in a journal, in the backyard of our first house. We are sitting shoulder to shoulder on a couch holding the contract for the first and only book we would write together. And those wedding pictures, mostly unposed, taken by a friend, both of us in white, grinning. Here we are flanking the Eiffel Tower. Here we are in Iceland. Here we are on a beach in California. It ends with that image, the two of us entwined with the Pacific behind us.

I know I must have looked at this video back when he sent it in July of 2019, but I have no memory of that. This viewing feels like the first time. The images are in no order. There is no narrative arc to this story Tom has put together to celebrate our married life. As I watch, and watch again, and again, I think about the ups and downs of a long marriage, about plateaus that seem endless, about dips that feel as if the bottom will fall out, about the surprise ascents. And it just keeps going. I think about Tom culling through hundreds and hundreds of photos to create this. I think about his choice of a song. Decades before this anniversary, when our relationship was less than a year old, and Tom was headed off to an internship at (oh, the irony) the National Cancer Institute, I had put together a mixtape for him. "Crazy Love" was the first song. But mostly, standing in front of my monitor, transfixed, watching our history unfold, I think about how very surprised I am not to feel sad. In fact, I feel joyous. This man loved me. I loved this man. So *this* is positivity bias. This is not a weight to carry. It is an unburdening of weight. Or at least it is a glimpse of a new way of inhabiting widowhood.

I didn't know the two nights we spent in a fancy suite in a downtown hotel would be our last outing together. It is early fall: crisp mornings, cloudless skies, the leaves on the backyard trees turning orange and yellow and red. The life-ending medications had arrived in the mail a few days before. He had opened the small box, examined the contents, studied the many pages of instructions, and packed it all back up, neatly, in the little box. The box sits on the mantel in the living room, where he sleeps on the hospital bed. Out the window, he can see one of the white oaks, its leaves the color of cinnamon. There is no discussion about when he will take the medicine. There is, for both of us, I think, relief that this is now all under his control. No more interviews with physicians, no more forms to fill out, no more check-ins from hospice workers, no more waiting periods. Just us. Just him. I don't know what he was thinking. I don't know if he had already chosen a date, or if he was waiting for some aha moment, or more likely, because of his long attention to dreams and their meanings, waiting for his unconscious to speak.

It is October 1. He has reserved a two-room suite on the top floor in a newly opened hotel. He has booked an in-room massage and is trying to arrange for an in-room barber. I understand the massage, the possibility of relaxation and release, the desire to feel physical pleasure at a time when almost nothing is physically pleasurable. The barber appointment stumps me at the time. Tom's hair had grown back after chemo, but it was hardly luxuriant—it never had been—and certainly not long enough to be shaggy. Maybe it was the normalcy of it? Maybe, it occurs to me now, he was preparing his body for its end, like the rituals practiced in many of the world's religions. Whatever the underlying reasons, if there were underlying reasons, I knew these in-room appointments were not so much a rich-person treat, and not a reaction to COVID—still at that time a real threat with more than 170,000 new cases every day—but rather because every other breath he took ended in a cough, and his feet and legs were too swollen for him to walk more than a few steps.

The suite is lovely, decorated not in generic hotel style but, as they say, bespoke. It seems odd to take note of this, given the circumstances, but I do. We have stayed in many places, my husband and I, from fleabag motels (with fleas) to tents and yurts to, once, a four-star hotel in Sorrento. I think it is good and important, somehow, that this is a very nice place. The bedroom is separated from an expansive living area by solid wooden sliding doors, which means he can be as comfortable as it is possible for him to be, and I can sleep on the couch with my noise-canceling earbuds. There's a little kitchen and a large dining table, on the center of which is a striking flower arrangement, the colors deep blue and bright yellow, like the sky, like the autumn leaves. I think it is part of the hotel's welcome "package," but it isn't. Tom has ordered it for me. He has used some of his small store of energy to set this up. I am speechless.

We settle in. The afternoon is slow and quiet. The sun streams in the floor-to-ceiling, south-facing windows. Tom naps. I try to read. Toward dinnertime, the children arrive. The boys, that is. Lizzie is not driving in from the coast. I don't know why. Jackson comes with his partner, carrying a gift basket they've put together—massage oils, a bath bomb, sleep gummies, chocolates. Zane and his wife arrive with fourteen-month-old Henry, whose energy immediately, deliciously fills the room. Liza, our daughter-in-law, hands the baby to my husband, who gathers him in his arms and slowly walks to the big window. He stands there for a long moment, one arm hooked under the baby's bottom, the other outstretched, pointing south, over downtown to the forested butte five miles distant. Our land is just on the other side of that butte. Tom is pointing to where we live, to where the baby's father and uncle and aunt grew up, but it seems clear—and not at all cheesy to imagine—that he is pointing to the future. Henry's future. The future he will inhabit without this grandfather.

I remember this scene with clarity, not just because the two of them were so still and silent, so intent on the experience, so much united in this moment, but also because I found my phone and captured the image. Later, more than two years later, Liza, who is a supremely talented artist, used the photograph to create a small, impressionist illustration, part of a show she had at a local gallery. Zane framed it. It sits on the windowsill of my bedroom, the first thing I see when I open my eyes.

That evening, we sit together at the big table and eat take-out food from a nearby fish-and-chips joint. Lizzie's absence is palpable. None of us speaks about it. When Tom goes back to the bedroom to nap, the boys and I go down to the lobby to talk about how to get Lizzie to come home, how to not guilt her but motivate her. She needs to be here. She will regret not being here. It is hard for me to imagine that Tom does not feel the sting of her absence, but maybe he doesn't. He was always able to let go of expectations in a way I could not, and now I think this is ever more so. But for the health of our family, for the future of us, I want us all to be together as the end to the old us approaches. The line between encouraging and guilting is, however, a thin one. I cross it all the time. I need help. I ask the boys to reach out, in their separate ways, however they deem best, to get Lizzie to come home. My efforts have not succeeded; otherwise, she would be with us right now.

I now know that my efforts failed, because when I talked to Lizzie on the phone, when I messaged and emailed her, I thought I was interacting with the old Lizzie, my tough, sometimes sweet, often mercurial, stubborn, bighearted daughter, Lizzie BA (Before Addiction). I was angry at that old Lizzie for what I perceived to be her willful separation from us, her selfishness, or maybe her laziness. I did not know the depth or width or breadth—whatever the measurement might be—of her addiction. I knew she was not in a happy place. I knew she was jumping from job to job. But back then, I still think I understand her, that she is still the girl whom I know.

She isn't.

Although Tom and I have read so many books and had so very many conversations about drug abuse, although we have seen a counselor and repeatedly tried to get Lizzie to talk to someone, we do not understand—we did not then understand—that our daughter, and her brain, were struggling with addiction. That the very chemistry of her brain had changed. We do not know that the change is not just the outsize response of pleasure receptors, the overstimulation of those receptors, the need for more and more. Her brain has changed in ways that affect focus, memory, learning, decision-making, and judgment. Now I know. To get smarter too late is a wound that may never heal.

The boys set up a group call with Lizzie. Tom is fitfully asleep. I leave the hotel to go walk by the river.

21

LIZZIE IS HEADED SOMEWHERE—we do not know where—driving her car, FA in the passenger seat. By the time we arrive at the beach house, Tom driving almost recklessly on winding two-lane roads, it has been more than three hours since I received the *FA here pounding the door* text. We drive straight to the tiny police office just off the main street. The clerk sitting behind the counter, a middle-aged woman, a stranger, gets up to hug me. The cop who's been texting and calling us is there with no news to share. He is apologetic. He is solicitous. He wishes there were something more he could do. He does make a call to the state police for us, connects us with the patrolman who stopped Lizzie's car. We get the same story we already know. He repeats that he talked to Lizzie separately, away from FA. But without her saying she was in trouble, and without FA "in the system," there was nothing they could do. They had to let them go.

Tom tells the state cop that we want to file a missing person's report. We field a series of questions. I find a recent photo of Lizzie on my phone and text it over.

We drive the four blocks from the police station to our little house. On the front door, there are imprints of the sole of a shoe. There are scuff marks on the living room wall. Upstairs, the door to her bedroom is off its hinges, the knob is in pieces in the hallway. We are putting together a narrative of what happened here. We scour the little house looking for clues about where they might be headed. Maybe Lizzie scribbled a note? Left a book opened to a page, a coded message? The only unusual thing we see, on a side table by the couch, is a long, narrow glass pipe with a round glass bowl at the end of it. There are scorch marks around the bowl.

We walk up and down our one-block street, knocking on neighbors' doors to ask if they've seen or heard anything. We know one of our neighbors quite well, an older female couple who've taken an interest in Lizzie and have occasionally invited her over for dinner on their back deck. They aren't home. No one else on the street has seen or heard anything. It is getting late.

Tom suddenly realizes we can track her phone through an app we all have on our family plan. This gives us hope, but only for a moment. Either her phone is turned off or out of power. Or maybe FA smashed it. We go by the local police station again to ask our cop friend if he has any ideas about what we can do. The local police are clearly invested in what is going on. Things like this don't happen in this quiet town of eight hundred, where crime is limited to an occasional break-in of someone's vacant summer home. The officer promises to call with any news. He suggests we wait at the house that night in case they head back. We don't know what else to do. Everything is immediate and real and at the same time like a bad dream from which we will awaken.

The next day, on the way back home, maybe an hour into the three-and-a-half-hour trip, I get a text. Connectivity is spotty on this drive. Until we get much closer to home, over the coast range and back into the valley, we often have no phone service at all. The text is from our hometown neighbors. We've known these folks for years. We know each other's children; we pet-sit for each other.

"Lizzie is at our house," the message reads.

It is close to another hour before I am able to communicate back. My neighbor reports that Lizzie showed up at their doorstep, pale and shaking, that morning. She was in "bad shape," my neighbor says, but immediately reassures me that my daughter is not ill, but rather just exhausted, stressed, maybe, the neighbor ventures gently, "hungover." Lizzie hasn't said much to them, only that she walked down to our house first but all the doors were locked, and she didn't have the key. She is asleep on their couch. We are still an hour away from home. It is a very long hour.

We pick up Lizzie at the neighbors' house. She is red-eyed, ghostly. Her arms are bruised. Her clothes are filthy. We want to know everything. She is not ready to talk. She is in a place we cannot reach. She sleeps for close to eighteen hours. Then she tells us what happened.

FA had appeared on the front porch of the house into which Lizzie had moved to get away from him, to make a new life. She says she has no idea how he found out where she was living. She had changed her phone number and, she said, had not posted anything on social media. I can only guess that she was communicating with someone who knew FA and that this person had passed the information to him. How did he manage to get out to the beach house? He had no car, no license. She doesn't know. These are details we don't care about. She didn't want to let him in, she says. She was scared. But he pounded on the door and then kicked it. Now she was afraid he'd damage the house, our house. She says she unlocked the door but ran upstairs to her bedroom and locked that door. We had seen the evidence of what happened up there. *You sent me to jail*, he yells at her. *You fucked up my life.* She says he threatened not just her but us, her family.

They fight. She is strong, my daughter, but not strong enough. He has a knife. That glass pipe we noticed on the end table in the living room of the beach house? It was not a weed pipe; I know this now. It was for smoking meth. They got high. She doesn't tell this part of the story.

He grabs her phone, her wallet. He forces her into the car. She tells us about the state cop stopping them, how she wanted to say something, but she was too scared. She tells about FA sitting in the passenger seat holding a knife in his hand, the point pressing against her thigh. She drove 175 miles like this, back to where FA was living, the place Lizzie called a "shack." It was late. He started drinking. He drank himself into a deep sleep. She watched him. She waited. Then, before dawn, she sneaked out of the house—no phone, no money—and walked the eight miles back to our home.

A week later, when she has rested, I take her to the domestic violence services clinic in town, where she meets with a counselor. She has refused to press criminal charges because she fears that even if he does go to jail again, when he gets out, he will find her, and he will hurt her. This is what, the research shows, so often prevents women from pressing charges: the fear of repercussions, the fear that taking action will only make things worse. The counselor tries to persuade Lizzie to at least file for a restraining order to prevent FA from "intimidating, molesting, interfering with, or menacing" her. The thirty-six months of probation he was serving, the legal ruling that mandated "no contact of any kind," was apparently an unenforceable "bench" probation that did not include supervision or check-ins and was not entered into a criminal record that cops could access. That's why his name didn't pop up when the cops stopped the car and ran a check. She needs the protection of a restraining order, the counselor tells her. She tells the counselor, and then me, that he will be furious if she does this, that he will "completely lose it" and come after her.

We talk this through at home. I know Tom wants to say, but doesn't, *How could it get any worse?* We make a plan that Lizzie will stay here at the house and that we will install a new security system. Both of us work mostly from home. She will not be alone.

I take her to the courthouse, where she meets privately with a victims' services counselor who helps her fill out a seven-page petition that documents, in details she has not previously shared with us, the specifics of the abuse and the violence. She allows me to read the report. I think she wants me to know without talking any more about it, without answering my questions. She wants me to tell Tom so she doesn't have to. A few days later, the judge approves the restraining order, and soon thereafter, she is notified that FA has been served. I am not sure Lizzie feels any safer, but I do think she feels mentally tougher. She has taken action. She has, in an important sense, taken control.

Two months after he is served with the restraining order, FA commits a crime, a robbery. We learn about this because we are signed up to receive alerts about his status. For beating up my daughter, he received a ninety-day sentence in county jail. For breaking into a house—unarmed, when no one was home—and stealing whatever it is he stole, he gets sentenced to eighteen months in prison. We are simultaneously appalled at the disparity and overjoyed that he will be in a cell for the next year and a half and not in our daughter's life. She starts getting better sleep. Her skin clears up. She begins to talk about the future.

Because there is a shortage of beds in other facilities, FA will be serving his term in the state's only maximum-security prison. It so happens that I am a volunteer at this prison. I had started a writers' group for lifers there, helping them find their voices, helping them to use writing to better understand their lives. For several years, I had been facilitating sessions inside the prison every other week.

I had not told the men in the group about my daughter. In the extensive training I went through to become an official volunteer, we were repeatedly instructed not to share personal information. It could be used against us, we were told. Manipulative inmates would find a way. I bristled at this injunction, first because the men were sharing emotionally intimate stories with me through their writing—they trusted *me*—and then, as time went on, because I came to know them as ethical people who would never game me.

So, when I learned that the man who had punched, kicked, bit, and terrorized my daughter, who had hunted her, tracked her down, held her hostage—*that man*—was now housed at the prison where I had ten "friends," I thought about revenge. I was going to tell the men in the group about my daughter's assailant and, in an open-ended but clearly malevolent way, ask if there was anything they could do to make his life inside a little worse. He harmed her. I wanted him to be harmed.

On my next visit to the prison to facilitate the writers' group, I arrived at our assigned room deep in the bowels of the penitentiary a few minutes early and saw that one of the men was already there. He was my most talented writer and a leader within the prison community. Forty years old, he had been behind bars since he was sixteen. He had taken a life, and it looked as if he would be spending all the rest of his life paying for that. As if there could be a "payment."

I told him about the abuse. I told him about the short jail sentence. I told him about the prison term, six times longer, for a nonviolent, victimless crime. I heard the anger in my voice. I felt the constriction in my chest. Then I told him I was going to ask the group to, essentially, exact revenge on my behalf. I didn't know what that might mean, but I had seen enough gritty black-and-white prison movies to imagine a beating out in the yard or a quick injury inflicted by a shiv fashioned from the end of a toothbrush.

Physical contact is forbidden between volunteers and inmates, but in this unguarded moment—literally unguarded: there was no guard present in the room—my prison writer reached out and very lightly placed his hand on my forearm. The touch was neither unwanted nor uncalled for, but it was, we both knew, a punishable offense. "Take time to think about it," he said. His tone was so very different from mine that it was startling, this man who'd come of age in prison, who had done bad things, who had seen bad things. He was calm. He was reasonable. "Don't put it out to the group yet," he advised, "and let me do a little research." I didn't know what he meant by "research," but I trusted his advice. He knew the world behind bars, and he knew the men in the group.

Two weeks later, when I returned to the prison for another writers' workshop, my anger, my maternal fury, had not dissipated. It was mixed with grief, the heartache of not having been able to protect my daughter from harm, and with dread for the possibility of future physical abuse. The writers' session zipped along with what had become our usual/unusual combination of soul-baring and dark humor, our toggling between the searing intimacy of the stories the men read aloud and the hilarious debates about the worst meal ever eaten behind bars. I didn't have the opportunity to talk with the man I had confided in until the group disbanded, and we were all heading to the stairs that led down to the main part of the prison. The men stood in line to have their IDs scanned by the guard. This man held back. "Listen," he said. "I want to tell you what I found out about the guy who beat up your daughter."

After a quarter of a century inside the walls, my informant knew the culture and operated within it like the native he was. "When you are going to move against somebody, you have to know who they are, how they are connected," he told me.

Although the prison housed more than two thousand men, he easily found the man who abused my girl and discovered, he said, that he was "a nobody." Back when he was in county jail serving time for domestic violence, this guy was "pumped," which meant he was tested by others, goaded to see what he would do. The test was simple: Someone took his food. He did nothing. Someone else took his food. Again, nothing. The conclusion was that he could be pushed around. He wouldn't stand up for himself. This bit of jailhouse intelligence followed him into the penitentiary, and anyone who might offer protection or a sense of belonging to a new guy wanted no part of him. But there might be others who *did* want a part of him. When my inside source told me that this guy was "scared and alone," I felt a rush of pleasure. Good: Let him be scared. Let him be very scared.

"If you want something to happen to this guy, it can happen," my inmate writer said. "But once you put that energy out in the world, it will always come back."

He was right, this man who did so much wrong. Of course he was. As soon as he said it, I got it. Wishing harm on someone who harmed was piling ugliness on top of ugliness. This behavior might work for a lioness on the savanna, but it was not a maternal act I wanted to model for my daughter. It was enough that she was out of danger. It was enough that he was being punished again for something.

Lizzie, who looks better, who says she feels better, who seems to *be* better, goes back to the beach house. Tom and I drive over to help her settle back in. I deep-clean the place. We sand and paint the door, repair the living room wall, install a new doorknob. Lizzie finds another culinary job and settles back in. After a while, she meets a new guy. We meet him on one of our now-monthly visits to check on her—visits masquerading as weekend outings to enjoy the town and the ocean. He is a few years younger, quiet, serious. He graduated from culinary school and works full-time as a cook at the dive bar Lizzie used to work at a half dozen jobs ago. He seems to be slowly transforming the kitchen from a burger-taco-nachos operation into something resembling a modest restaurant. He tries out new recipes for Lizzie. He has a complicated backstory—don't we all?—so he fits the mold of Lizzie choosing friends whom she thinks she can "fix." But he is holding a steady job, and he has a gentle voice, and the bar has been set so low with FA that this guy seems to us like Prince Charming. I think, watching them laugh, and talk, and work together making a complicated meal in the little kitchen in the beach house, that her life may be turning around.

22

THERE ARE FIVE KINDS of rain today: moderate rain, heavy rain, downpour, deluge, and torrent. There are four kinds of mountain ascents today: muddy with slippery leaves, muddy with rocks, muddy and rocky with cow pies, and ludicrous. The ascent is an unremitting 5-mile climb with an elevation gain of more than 2,600 feet, all part of an epic 23-mile, 10-hour hiking comedy of errors day. This day, my 25th on the Camino, makes the ascent to the Cruz de Ferro seem like a romp, and that reputed this-is-the-toughest-it-gets first day over the Pyrenees not even worth a mention. I am not whining. I may be cursing, but I am not whining. I am acutely aware that I am choosing this challenge. I remind myself (yet again) that being able to choose the challenge, experiencing that sense of control when so much that has happened in my life, in our lives, is out of our control, is empowering. That thought is, in fact, powering me up this arduous climb in the Cantabrian Mountains. The physicality of it, the sweaty, drenching work of it, demands my attention. Which means, for most of this very, very long day, I do not think about what I left beneath the iron cross a few days ago and whether that pilgrim ritual, which means so much to so many, will have lasting meaning for me.

The goal today is the tiny mountain village of O Cebreiro, population 26, perched at 4,265 feet at the crest of the mountain range that borders the region of Galicia, which is known as the "green Spain" due to its lush landscapes, fertile soils, and, yes, frequent rainfall. The tough five-mile climb to this ancient village will come at the end of an already long day of walking. The question, pondered the day before, is whether to make the climb at the end of that long day or, like many pilgrims choose to do, stop at a village before the big ascent and climb first thing in the morning. I am with Kiki, and we decide we don't want to wake up to a daunting morning. We will hike all the way through to O Cebreiro and stay there that night. It will be demanding, but we remind each other of the Meseta marathon we conquered, and that, separately and together, we have already walked more than 375 miles since the start of this trek.

It's one thing to decide and another to make it happen. The initial obstacle is that we can't find any open beds in O Cebreiro. There aren't many options. We are using multiple apps, cross-checking, WhatsApp-ing when we can find a phone number, coming up with nothing. Then, oddly, we find a mention of a place on one of the apps, a place that is not listed elsewhere.

There's no way to cross-check or look at reviews, but there is a phone number. Kiki, who has both a phone that works and much better Spanish than I do—two attributes in addition to her dark humor and vast knowledge of literature that have endeared her to me since the first afternoon we met—makes the call and, we think, secures us two beds.

We start walking together that morning before dawn, slogging through the aforementioned (and in no way exaggerated) awful weather, traipsing through dense forests and open farmlands and cow pastures, and plodding up that final five-mile-long climb. Eight hours later, we make it to the top. The view down into the lush valleys of Galicia is stunning. But there is nothing at all up here at the top, just a stone wall and two dirt paths. Kiki fires up her iPhone and connects to Google Maps to locate our accommodations. The map shows that the place is not in O Cebreiro proper but rather in a town called Pedrafita do Cebreiro, four kilometers away. Four kilometers is only two and a half miles, but when you've already walked close to twenty miles, and when the last three hours of the hike have been a rocky, muddy climb, four more kilometers seems like a long, long way. We are not happy. We have no choice but to continue on.

The first part of the walk is a steep descent alongside a two-lane highway. Now Google Maps takes us up above the highway on what seems to be a narrow logging road that leads to an even narrower path, a track through the grass, maybe a shepherd's trail. There is no signage. There are no fellow hikers. But there is rain. And anxiety. The path dips down, snakes through the woods, and finally, just when anxiety is about to become panic, empties out onto a paved street. We have reached our destination, this other town with a name confusingly similar to the village we thought we'd be staying at. Kiki starts to check Google Maps to locate our place, but there is no need. At the entrance to the town is a mural-size decorative map. Our accommodation is marked by a dot. It is just down the road, minutes away.

We start walking. There is just one main street to this less-than-charming town, and that street is a two-lane thoroughfare for delivery trucks. The street is lined with small garages, automotive repair shops, gas stations, and empty storefronts. We walk to the address we have, the one listed on the app, the one marked on the welcoming map at the entrance to town. There is nothing. Not only is there no albergue; that address, that street number, doesn't exist. We backtrack, cross the street, check again. We decide we must have it wrong. We walk back up the four or five blocks to the entrance to town and stare at the map. We had the number right. There's a Twilight Zone vibe to all this. How can the city map show something that doesn't exist? How can Google Maps direct us to a nonexistent place?

Kiki goes back to working her phone. I walk down a narrow side street, find a small bakery, and, in halting Spanish, ask the woman behind the counter about our albergue. She shakes her head. I've probably communicated badly. I try again, showing her the picture I took on my phone of the city map. I zoom out and point at the name of the albergue and the dot marking the spot. "*Aquí no*," she says. Not here. "*¿Dónde?*" I ask. She shakes her head again, this time more vigorously. "*No conozco el lugar*," she says. My high school Spanish kicks in. She is telling me she doesn't know this place. She tells me she has lived here her whole life and "*este lugar no está aquí*." This place is not here.

I find Kiki standing in front of the map, alternately staring at it and her phone. I relate the conversation with the bakery woman. *Flummoxed* is a wonderful and not-often-used word. We are flummoxed. We are also soaked and tired and have long exhausted our seemingly inexhaustible store of bad jokes, nut sack references, and rah-rah pep talks. Kiki gets on Booking.com and finds us a room in a place that we think actually exists in this town. We walk down that same diesel-scented street to a nondescript building with the correct address. It looks like a small apartment house that has seen better days. There's no signed entrance, no lobby, just a touchpad near a small, locked door. Kiki reads the instructions and pushes the buttons. We can make out a voice at the other end but not what the voice is saying. There is a buzz. The small door unlocks. We walk in and are faced with a long, dark flight of stairs. We walk up to the first floor. There is a locked door at the landing. We walk up to the second floor. There is a locked door at the landing. We stand there together, frozen between laughing and crying. This day is overflowing with bad surprises. Where is this albergue or hostel or whatever the hell it is?

"*¡Hola!*" Kiki yells up into the stairwell. Silence. She yells louder. Then I yell. We hear a faint voice. "*Arriba*," it says. Then, "*Tercer piso.*" Kiki translates, "Third floor," although I understand. We climb another set of stairs. And there, at the top, is a young woman standing behind a tiny counter, smiling at us.

I wish the story ended there on the third floor of this slightly sketchy building in this truck thoroughfare of a town with us finding our beds, shedding our wet ponchos and our soaked hiking shoes, and taking a breath and settling in. But it doesn't. Because as we are signing the roster, it occurs to me that I have no idea where my bag is, my backpack that I chose to send ahead that day to give my collarbone bruise a rest. I had filled out a tag the night before with the name of the albergue (the one that seems not to exist), attached it to my backpack, and set it out for the transport "company"—a.k.a. some local guy with a car—to pick up. Where could *mi mochila* possibly have been delivered? How can I find it? What will I do without it? The fact that this has happened before doesn't give me solace. This is too complicated a situation to express to the young woman behind the counter, who knows no English. We use a combination of halting Spanish, hand signals, pictures on our phones, and a translation app to explain all this.

The young woman nods vigorously. She picks up her phone and makes a call to the transport company—that is, the local driver—to see what she can find out for us. The driver, who also apparently delivers mail and offers a taxi service and maybe is her cousin, remembers my backpack. Yes, he tells the young woman, he delivered it to its destination in O Cebreiro earlier that day. The *destination*? So, my backpack is four kilometers back up the mountain at the place that Google Maps told us wasn't there? I don't get it. But I am thrilled to know it is somewhere. Maybe he can go get it and deliver it to me here? That's one idea. But that would mean waking up tomorrow and climbing back up the side of the mountain, the one we hiked down just now, to meet up with the Camino. A better idea is for him to come to where we are, get us, and drive us to where the backpack is. Meanwhile, this young woman, who probably thinks we are silly, clueless norteamericanos (and is not far from wrong), is patiently and sweetly helping us.

Maybe because this place at the top of the stairs looks so charmless, maybe because we are now overwhelmed with curiosity about actually finding the albergue we couldn't find, mostly because we don't want to climb again tomorrow, we hire the bag transporter–mailman–taxi driver–cousin to pick us up and take us back to O Cebreiro. We wait on the sidewalk, in the rain, for twenty-five minutes. The drive back up the mountain takes four minutes. Walking it would have taken us an hour and a half. The man drops us off on the back side of the tiny village, not where the Camino path led us a few hours earlier, but probably down one of those dirt paths we saw when we got to the top and did not explore. The car stops in a courtyard in front of a charming old stone building. The name of this place is similar to, but not the same as, the one we couldn't find. This explains what happened and makes us feel less crazy than we were feeling.

Miraculously, although it is after six, our reservation is still good. Miraculously, my pack is sitting next to the check-in desk. Even more miraculously, this place, which is dark and medieval and lovely, has a little restaurant. The hospitalero tells us, we think, that dinner starts at seven. This is early for Spain, and a wonderful surprise. We find our beds, take showers, scrounge around for something dry to wear, and present ourselves to be fed. As it turns out, we had misunderstood our host. She had told us that the restaurant would *close* at seven. It is 7:05. The best she can do is offer soup—Kiki orders this, and it never comes—and pizza. The pizza does come, clearly a frozen one from a supermercado, crust like cardboard, which we devour as if it were flown in fresh and hot from Napoli.

If "things happen for a reason," what was the reason for this exhausting, baffling, physically demanding, anxiety-ridden, dark comedy of a day? The self-help lit—which I have dabbled in more than I would like to admit—proclaims that challenges are opportunities for personal growth that teach valuable lessons and build resilience. To which I say, thanks, but I believe my challenges-that-test-my-mettle dance card is already full. Another idea is that experiences such as this can teach us about the interconnectivity of events, the chain reaction that is life, which helps us make sense of why things happen the way they do. The immediate lesson here is obvious and superficial: This whole fiasco began with and can be attributed to the difference between the actual name of the hostel and the name that appeared in the app we used. This does not explain the big, colorful city map, with its listing of the albergue that didn't exist at an address that didn't exist, but the map will forever defy explanation. Perhaps that is the lesson here: that sometimes what happens defies explanation. How else to understand the illness and death of my husband? How else to explain Lizzie's descent?

Another idea gleaned from the what-doesn't-kill-you-makes-you-stronger crowd is the realization that negative experiences can be interpreted as stepping stones to a larger, beneficial process. That is a hope I nourish as I navigate not just this Camino but my new life. It is a hope we all have to nourish, I think, as we continue to make our way through unsettling times, as we look for ways to build, not lose, strength. This is important. This is good. It is hard, purposeful work. Of course, making a story out of something, crafting a narrative of one's life, or a particular moment in one's life, brings coherence to what may appear to be chaos.

But there is something else going on here for me. I think about this all through the next day as Galicia unfolds, dazzlingly verdant, blindingly green, with the blessing of no rain and the curse of fifty-mile-an-hour wind gusts. I think: I no longer have a life partner, the one person with whom I have had so many experiences, some days that were magical, other days that were hellish. And so, the intimacy and urgency and intensity of the O Cebreiro day with Kiki is both sweet and bitter to me. She and I lived it together. We shared the adventure, the confusion, the relief. And the sharing is important. The sharing made it not only bearable but, at just the moments most needed, laughable. I don't know if Kiki and I will remain friends. She lives half a continent away. I may never see her after this journey is over. But we will both tell this tale, each in our own way. Our friendship will live on through this telling. My ability to feel this connection, the power and depth of it, suggests that maybe I am not as armored as I used to be.

23

HOW DOES SOMEONE BECOME a meth addict?

Quickly.

Maybe even unwittingly.

There's that first time—Was it with FA? Was it in some guy's apartment after the bars closed? Even earlier than that?—that first rush, the power of it, the way everything, everything—what you say, what you do, doing nothing, saying nothing—everything feels so good. And it's all suddenly clear to you. What is clear? Everything. Every sensation is amplified. Every moment is imbued with significance. Everything is brighter, more vibrant, more interesting. Including you. What worried you, does not. The demons that whispered in your ear, that appeared in your dreams? They are banished. You are smart, smarter than you ever thought you were. You are self-assured. You are invincible. You vibrate with pleasure. The euphoria, that first time, must feel like the hand of God on your forehead.

But it isn't. It is the drug causing a massive release of dopamine, the chemical messenger, the neurotransmitter associated with pleasure and reward. It is the drug elevating another neurotransmitter, norepinephrine, which heightens alertness and sharpens focus. And it is the rush of serotonin, the chemical messenger that signals happiness and optimism. The brain remembers this euphoric surge and associates it with the drug.

If it feels this good, why wouldn't you do it again? And again? Meanwhile, the brain's circuits are quickly adapting to the drug, becoming less sensitive to the chemical messengers, needing more and more to create the same surge. Would you know—would you care—that what you are doing is severely, possibly forever, altering the chemistry of your own brain? Would you know that what you are doing is making it harder and harder for your brain to make those same chemicals that cause you to feel so good, that the drug is killing neurons, shrinking brain volume, that if you keep doing what you're doing, you can suffer cognitive decline, that this drug that enhanced clarity, attention, pleasure, and confidence can forever impair your ability to feel those feelings without the drug?

If it feels this good, and it takes a little more of the drug to achieve the high, and then a little more, and then a little more, so be it. If getting high is what you think about when you wake up; if, when you deplete your stash and you need more and you start sweating and feeling anxious and maybe imagining things, do you think of yourself as an addict? Or is this just life now?

I am not an addict. I was the mother of one. What I think I understand now is *how* she became an addict, the neurobiology of it, the clear biochemical path to dependency. What I understand is that addiction is a brain disease. What I understand is that, as the disease took hold, she was not making "bad choices," or conscious, rational decisions. Her brain, altered by the drug, was not functioning this way.

I have researched my way into this understanding of the how. The knowledge does not relieve the pain; it does not help the healing, but it does take away some of the confusion, especially the part of me that questioned, at the time, how she could make such bad choices. Missing work. Coming in late so often she got fired. Yelling at a boss in front of patrons (I have not related that story). Not taking care of the house. Her car. Her health. Maybe, even, although I am loath to consider this, letting FA know where she was when she left town to escape him. These were not choices. They had ceased to be choices. This was not my girl living her life. This was the drug controlling her life. I see this in hindsight. I don't know if it would have made a difference in real time. Her long talks with us, with Tom in particular, ended in promises never kept. Her resistance to therapy was unwavering.

If I didn't understand the how as it was happening, I certainly did not understand—and still struggle to understand—the why. Why did my girl become an addict? What I saw at the time, or what blinded me from really seeing, or what caused me to underestimate (or deny) what I did see was this: I saw a girl, a young woman, born with privilege. Not summer-house-in-the-Hamptons privilege. But privilege nonetheless. She was white, cisgender, healthy. She had parents who loved her and showed it; older brothers who doted on her; a grandfather who adored her; aunts who pampered her. She grew up in a safe home—no alcohol, no drugs, no drama. Her own room. Nutritious and abundant food. She grew up in a safe environment—clean air, clean water, low crime. She grew up with people cheering for her, literally and otherwise.

There was every reason, based on that naive checklist I had in my mind, for her to have a smooth path through life. She did, early on and consistently, choose friends who had big issues, friends whose lives were full of the drama hers was not. I thought these choices—and back then, they *were* choices—and the way she listened to the tales of others, and how she wanted to help, might mean that as she grew, she would become a therapist or a counselor. I remember a conversation in the car one afternoon when she told me about an idea she had to combine baking and therapy. She was then just out of high school, working part-time at a bakery and taking a few classes at the community college. She had just learned about "walk and talk" therapy in a required human relations class.

"No one wants to talk about themselves when someone is staring at them," she said. I laughed. This was precisely why our deepest conversation happened in the car while I was driving, my eyes straight ahead. It was also one of the many complaints Lizzie had about her several counseling sessions back in high school, the ones she was forced to attend after the vodka-in-the-water-bottle incident. "So, suppose, like, I was kneading dough at a big table and talking with someone about their life and their issues at the same time." I nodded, careful to keep my eyes on the road. "They would feel all relaxed, right? It would just feel like talking." I thought this was brilliant and told her so. She was thoughtful and imaginative and got excited about plans. And then the plans never happened.

Because Lizzie was who she was, because we were who we were, because none of this fit the image I had of "addict," I didn't see her as one—would never have used this word—even when the evidence was there. I wonder how much of my own ego blocked this realization. What kind of a mother raises a daughter who becomes an addict? My blindness, Tom's too, I would also attribute to my daughter's fierce and stubborn spirit. Of all the things I loved about her, this was right at the top. She was strong, and she was strong-willed. After all that had happened with FA, after her seeming recovery at home, after her resettling in the beach house, finding another job, connecting with a new boyfriend, she seemed strong.

But there are limits to strength, to hers and to all of ours. In the spring of 2020, she and the new boyfriend both lost their culinary jobs. Pandemic shutdowns walloped the hospitality industry (8.2 million workers lost their jobs), and little towns that depended on tourists and vacation rentals like the beach community they lived in shut down almost completely. Oregon's lockdowns were particularly strict, but several coastal towns went even further than the governor's mandates, issuing emergency orders that closed hotels, motels, and vacation rentals to discourage visitors. Public access to beaches and parks was restricted. After a few months, some services reopened, but strict mask mandates, social distancing, limitations on the size of gatherings—and the fears we all had about being in enclosed spaces—meant that jobs like Lizzie's did not bounce back. She remained unemployed for a long time, existing on funds we put in her bank account and SNAP benefits. She got COVID, recovered, got COVID again. I drove out several times to see her. We wore masks in the house. We didn't hug. The isolation out there was extreme. The town, minus the visitors who supported the restaurants she had worked in, had barely eight hundred people. I wanted her to come home. She wouldn't consider it. She said she'd be fine. She said she was coping. But as the saying goes: "Just because I carry it doesn't mean it's not heavy."

It was heavy.

What I didn't know, what Lizzie didn't know—what several million of us found out after reading Bessel van der Kolk's best-selling treatise on trauma, *The Body Keeps the Score*—is that *the body keeps the score.* Her body was keeping score, even as she moved forward, or maybe pretended to move forward in her life. X-rays and scars would show the consequences of the physical trauma she suffered. But just as methamphetamine was changing the structure of her brain, so, too, was the trauma she suffered and the dislocation and anxiety that were part of the pandemic experience. This embodiment of trauma is the thesis of the book, a book I read more than a year too late. I may be wrong, but I don't think it was physical beatings that left her traumatized. She took action then. She regained some control. He went to jail. And the physical wounds she suffered were wounds you could see. They were wounds that healed.

But when he appeared on the porch of her "safe house," when he pounded on the door and kicked the wall and stripped the knob from her bedroom door, when he essentially kidnapped her, when the cops couldn't help, when he kept her locked in his house: This was the trauma that continued to live inside of her. And the trauma of her father's death lived inside her as well. The loss was and is felt deeply by all of us. But at the time, my sons and I worked together toward healing ourselves. We talked and remembered; we spent time together; we marked his day of death with Negronis toasted at dusk. We planned a farewell event for his close friends. Lizzie was distant and silent. She stayed away.

If Van der Kolk is right, these traumas—unresolved—had many consequences that made her life physically, psychologically, and emotionally more challenging than it already was. His inventory of these potential consequences is harrowing, and as I reread it now, I think back on the times we drove over to the coast to see Lizzie, and the texts we exchanged, and her resistance—that's how I thought of it, mistakenly—to coming home for visits, I can put check marks next to so many items on Van der Kolk's list, behaviors we saw but didn't see, what she did not let us see, what we explained away: generalized anxiety, avoidance of trauma reminders, loss of interest in activities, feelings of worthlessness, intense emotions and mood swings, impulsive behaviors, insomnia. And of course, hidden in plain view, was what she did to try to medicate it all away, what she did that allowed her, until it didn't, to carry the burden. One significant consequence of unresolved, embodied trauma is, in Van der Kolk's words, "increased reliance on alcohol, drugs, or other substances to cope with trauma symptoms."

More than 16.8 million people age twelve or older used or tried methamphetamine sometime during their lives, according to a 2021 National Survey on Drug Use and Health. In 2022, the year Lizzie had a new boyfriend and a new job, the year she carried her burdens the only way she knew how, more than 109,000 people died of drug overdoses in the US, many attributed to the use of a stimulant like methamphetamine plus an opioid like fentanyl. There's a quote misattributed to Josef Stalin that goes: "Thousands of deaths are a statistic. One death is a tragedy."

That tragedy, that year, was Lizzie.

24

THE MESSAGE COMES THROUGH Facebook at 3:23 p.m. on June 20. It is one of those perfect Oregon days—cerulean skies, mid-seventies, everything still blindingly green from a long, rainy spring. It's from GB, Lizzie's boyfriend.

Something happened to Liz please call me please it's an emergency.

My first thought is that she has gotten into a car accident. She was injured. How badly? How long will it take me to drive to whatever hospital she is at? Phone service out at my house, nestled in a hollow five miles out of town, is spotty. I go outside to sit on the grass alongside the driveway to make the call.

How did he tell me? Did he say, "Liz is dead"? Or did he ease into it? I don't remember. What I remember is feeling numb but also jittery. Breathless. Sick to my stomach. Everything at once and then nothing.

In that frozen moment, I don't know who I am. The words I am hearing seem to be part of some story that has no relation to me. I am just sitting there in the grass listening to some guy tell me someone is dead. This reaction, I learn later, is what those in the mental health field call *disassociation*, a natural response to shock, a way to cope with overwhelming emotions. You feel disconnected. You experience "derealization," the sense that the world is not real, that the experience itself stands outside reality. You, untethered, find yourself outside the scene you are in the midst of living. For me, there is another layer: I am not only an observer, I am also observing the self who is observing the scene. If this sounds hallucinogenic, that's exactly how it feels. What happens next is that the self being observed, the me that is not me, turns into a journalist investigating a story: inquisitive, emotionless.

I sit in the hot sun for a long time. I don't know how long. Time is not real either. A determined reporter, I pepper GB with questions. But he knows very little. He was not with her when whatever happened, happened. He tells me that Lizzie had left late the night before—at this point, they are living in GB's van parked in someone's driveway—to "go visit a new friend." GB says he didn't know who the friend was or where Lizzie went. She didn't return that night or the next morning. The journalist asks: *Weren't you concerned? What did you do?* The interview subject is crying too hard to answer. The hospital called him that afternoon. How did the hospital know to call him? Why didn't the hospital call "the mother"? This doesn't make sense. But nothing is making sense right now.

He tells me that when he got to the hospital, no one would talk to him—he had no standing—but apparently, someone did talk to him, because he was told she had died. He wasn't allowed to see her. But he was allowed to take a necklace she was wearing. I am confused about all of this, intent on understanding these small details that somehow feel important to the story I am busy reporting. He asks me twice, maybe three times, if it was okay for him to take the necklace. With the repeated mention of the necklace, I am drawn back to reality. I am no longer shielded, disassociated. I am again who I am: the mother of a child who was taken to a hospital, the mother of a child who has died. That necklace. I can see it. I'm sure it was the necklace I gave her for high school graduation, the silver spiral one with the hidden engraving that only she and I knew about, the one I designed and had a jeweler friend make for her. She always wore it.

GB doesn't know much, but he does know the name of the hospital. It's a small facility in a community twenty-five miles from where he and Lizzie have been living. It's designated as a trauma 4 center, which is lowest level of expertise, basic care, the place where they "stabilize" you and quickly send you off to a bigger, better hospital with a full range of specialists and sophisticated equipment. I look this up later as I go down the rabbit hole of *could she have been saved if she had been close to a trauma 1 hospital.*

There is nothing more he can tell me, nothing more I can say. But we can't seem to end the call. Lizzie is there, between us, a thread. Maybe we can't bear to break that connection. But I must. I find the number for the hospital, get connected to the ER, ask to speak to the doctor who treated Lizzie. I think there is only one ER doctor. I get his name. He will call back. I wait, sitting on the grass in the hot sun. When he returns the call, forty minutes later, he begins with the obligatory "I'm sorry for your loss." I wonder how many times this doctor has said these words. He seems to think this *sorry* statement is enough. It is not. I want to know everything that was done for her, everything that was done *to* her. Weeks later, I request all the records—ambulance, ER, medical examiner, toxicology report—hoping that the details will give me peace. They don't. On the phone, he hesitates to be specific. Maybe he figures I won't understand. Maybe he doesn't want to be talking to a woman whom he fears will become hysterical. There are a few things I am good at, and getting people to talk is one of them. Not falling apart in front of others is another.

This is what he says and what the reports later confirm: She arrived at the ER cyanotic—her skin was bluish purple—unconscious, unresponsive, with no heartbeat. In the ambulance, during the twenty-minute drive from the house of this "new friend" to the hospital, the paramedics had worked on her. They inserted an IV and delivered seven separate doses of epinephrine to try to get her heart to start beating. They gave her a whopping dose of Narcan—four times the standard measure—a medicine that, if administered in time, rapidly reverses an opioid overdose. They placed a breathing tube down her trachea, performed manual bagging to get oxygen into her. They administered CPR. They shocked her with a defibrillator. The ER doctor said the EMTs reported getting a very weak pulse at one point but lost it almost immediately.

At the hospital, the ER team continued resuscitation efforts, CPR, bagging. It had been more than an hour since the EMTs found her with no heartbeat, no blood circulating through her body, no nourishment to her brain. Looking later at the conflicting reports from the police who investigated her death and the hospital that recorded what was done and when, I think she had been without life for much longer than an hour. I think it may have been at least several hours before the woman, the "new friend" who lived in what the police told me was a "known drug house," noticed Lizzie comatose on the couch and called an ambulance. I imagine—of course I do not know—that this "friend," this supplier of drugs, was herself high. Maybe, I tell myself, it was a blessing—can that word be used?—that the EMTs and the ER team were unable to revive her. They "called it"—pronounced her dead—at 1:55 p.m. It chills me to think this; it nearly paralyzes me to write this: My daughter, if revived, would have almost assuredly been brain-dead.

Later, I try to imagine what happened the day she died. I know everything about Tom's death—the room, the time of day, the weather outside, what he said, what we said, what he was wearing, his breath as it quieted, the warmth of his hand in mine, sitting next to his body after he left it. I know almost nothing about Lizzie's, and it is the not knowing that haunts me. And so I try to reconstruct. On the ambulance report is the address of the house where she died. I drive three hours to that town, stop my car at the bottom of a hill, and walk up to the house. The concrete walkway is buckled, the weeds are high, the paint is peeling. I can't see into the house, because the front windows are covered with bedsheets. It looks like the kind of place someone would OD in. I consider knocking on the door. I don't. I just stand there for what seems like a long time but probably is not. Then I walk back down the hill, get in my car, and drive away.

The forensic report tells me just what she was wearing: a multicolored flannel shirt, a black sleeveless shirt, a gray bra, her signature ripped jeans. The report details her jewelry—her two necklaces, the ring around her left thumb, the black rubber bracelet I gave her with the inscription *You can do hard things*. Her fingernails, the report notes, were "dirty and unkempt." My Lizzie, the Lizzie before all that happened, happened—before FA, before drugs, before living in a van—loved to give herself manicures. She had beautiful hands, good strong nails. When she lived at home, her bathroom counter was cluttered with lotions and moisturizers, undercoats and topcoats, bottles of polish.

I know from the toxicology report what was in her system: the meth, the fentanyl. I assume she believed she was buying and smoking meth, her drug of choice (as if it were a choice any longer) and that the fentanyl was added. Drug dealers cut methamphetamine with fentanyl. This is all over the news. Fentanyl is up to fifty times more potent than heroin and one hundred times more powerful than morphine. Adding fentanyl creates a much more intense high. And it is cost-effective, as fentanyl is a relatively cheap drug to produce. I also know—this I researched after Lizzie's death—that drug overdoses largely caused by fentanyl reached record highs in the early 2020s. In 2022, the year Lizzie ODed, the Centers for Disease Control and Prevention reported that 73,654 people died of fentanyl overdoses. What I don't know is what it actually means to overdose. What happens to you? What does it feel like? What did Lizzie feel?

I have a friend I can ask. He is an ER doc. He is also a father whose son died of an overdose. This man whom I met several months after the deaths of our children is not just a fellow traveler down the road no parent wants to travel but also an extraordinary source of information, and maybe most important of all, a person who has never said, "I'm sorry for your loss," or that other, even less helpful and most common remark, "I can't imagine what this must feel like." He can imagine. And it is a relief to be around him, because there's so much we don't have to say.

I tell him about the ER report that notes "cardiac arrest." I tell him about the autopsy report that notes "severe cerebral edema." We are eating bowls of oatmeal at my favorite coffeehouse, talking about death and addiction but also about the right rudders of airplanes and the marauding deer that eat our respective landscapes and the lost craft of cobbling shoes. We have to shift from death to deer to loafers to make these conversations bearable. He tells me that when a person overdoses from an opioid, it is not the cardiac arrest that kills, nor is it the swelling of the brain. These are consequences, not causes. He says that the opioid depresses breathing. The brain would normally get the message that you now have too much carbon dioxide in your system, and you need to breathe. This is the signal you get when you swim underwater and are cued, with great urgency, to surface for breath. But the opioid also silences that signal in the brain. So, you are not cued. You do not resume normal breathing. The carbon dioxide builds. The breathing is further depressed. Then you stop breathing. It is respiratory arrest that kills you. I am taking notes on all this. Finally, he gets to the part I care about, the reason I asked the question.

"It is a calm death," he tells me. "You simply stop breathing. You have no consciousness that you need to breathe. There is no pain. There is just unconsciousness." This is eerily very much like Tom's death. One drug rendered him unconscious; the other stopped his breathing. But, of course, we were all with him. And he knew what he was doing. He chose this end for himself.

Now I know all the facts I will ever know about the circumstances of her death. Now I can put them together to imagine the scene. I have to imagine the scene. I need to be there: Lizzie in her carefully ripped jeans and her multicolored flannel shirt is sitting on a couch in that woman's rat shack of a place. She places the crystal meth in the glass pipe and taps the pipe gently to settle the rocks in the bowl. I know she smokes it. The autopsy report that detailed everything about her, inside and out, noted no needle tracks. And I saw the meth pipe in the living room of the beach house more than a year ago not knowing it was for meth, thinking it was for weed. She places a lighter under the bowl, careful not to let the flame touch the glass. She moves the lighter back and forth to distribute the heat evenly, watching as the crystals change to liquid, waiting for the vapor to rise. She inhales slowly and exhales immediately. She knows, because she has done this so very many times before, that holding the vapor in the lungs can cause burns and will not lead to a better high. She waits for the meth high, the high her body craves. It comes. But the meth is spiked with enough—more than enough—fentanyl to slow her breathing and drop her into unconsciousness. And then into breathlessness. She dies not knowing she is dying.

The county sheriff's office investigates the death. The day after sitting by the driveway in the sun talking to GB and then the ER doctor, I am talking to a detective. It helps that the detective is a woman. It helps that she is a mother. She doesn't say she is sorry for my loss. She tells me that a detective has interviewed the woman whose house Lizzie died in. On videotape, the woman says that she thought Lizzie was "sleeping in a bit too late." In attempting to arouse her, the woman noted "unusual secretions around the mouth" (that is, blood) and her "lack of breathing." The detective tells me the sheriff's office wants to see if they can mount a "Len Bias" case against the woman. She spends a while explaining this to me. She says that a number of states, Oregon being one of them, have adopted these so-called Len Bias laws, named after a college basketball star who died of a cocaine overdose. Later, I do my own research on the case and discover that Bias, who had just signed with the Boston Celtics, died in 1986 on June 20. June 20 is when Lizzie died. His death and the successful criminal trial mounted against the supplier of the drug that killed him led to the Anti-Drug Abuse Act of 1986. That act, the Len Bias Law, imposes severe penalties—a mandatory minimum of twenty years—on drug dealers if the drugs they sell result in the death of the user. I listen carefully to the detective. I get the sense that this case would be a very big deal for the law enforcement in this small town. I think about the whole "she would not have died in vain" trope if the woman is convicted. I wish it gave me comfort.

Much later, I find out from the detective that, when presented with the evidence gathered, the county DA declined to prosecute on those charges. She doesn't know why. The sheriff's office also referred charges against the woman for child neglect and reckless endangering of a minor. That's right. There was a minor, her son, in the house when my daughter ODed on the living room couch, when the ambulance came, when the EMTs worked on her, when she was taken away on a gurney. On this charge, she pled no contest and received a suspended sentence and eighty hours of community service. She got off easier than

FA, who broke Lizzie's ribs and cracked her vertebra and spent three months in county jail for the crime. At least Lizzie walked away from that.

Her body lies in the hospital for three days. There is some bureaucratic snafu or some debate about who will be doing the autopsy. I'm not sure, and I'm not getting good information. Finally, I hear that she is transported ninety miles to the state medical examiner's office, where the autopsy takes place. I call our local funeral home, the one just a few miles down the street, the one that knows me so well. It was just eight months ago that Tom was cremated there. I arrange for them to pick her up and bring her back home.

25

I HAVE BEEN ON the Camino for a month now. The days don't, as the expression goes, "fly by." They walk by. Ever since that four-minute taxi ride up the mountain from Do Cebreiro to O Cebreiro—a trek, in reverse, that took Kiki and me an hour and a half to navigate—I have been even more aware of the gloriously, occasionally maddeningly, slow pace of this journey. The glorious part is how this pace makes it possible to be without thought for long stretches, to achieve that meditative state I have rarely been able to achieve sitting cross-legged on the floor, trying so hard, too hard, to "observe thoughts" with "detached awareness" and "no judgment." I am spectacularly bad at this. But here, on the Camino, I fall into it with ease. The glorious part is how every day, although in some ways grindingly similar (wake, walk, eat, sleep), is also sprinkled with surprise. The maddeningly slow part comes with the weather. In mid-October, for four days during this last week I am on the Camino, Spain is hit by a severe weather system known as Storm Armand. It has a name, but it is not a hurricane, although it might as well be. Storm Armand brings torrential rains and wind gusts up to sixty-two miles an hour. I have walked through rain before. I have gotten very wet before. But this is megaweather. This is front-page-news weather. Walking through it—my shoes muddy and sodden, my poncho billowing like a sail and listing me port to starboard—time stands still. And in that stillness of time, I have lots of time for self-pitying thoughts, closely followed by ashamed thoughts for having self-pitying thoughts because, *querida peregrina* (I say to myself), *You chose this*. All this thinking is the opposite of that lovely meditative state I have experienced. Which makes me feel sorry for myself again. Which makes me feel ashamed of feeling sorry for myself. Until the rain lets up, at least for a while, as one front of the storm system passes through and another has not yet arrived, and I am overcome with gratitude for the calm.

I can now pay attention to the dazzling green countryside of Galicia and the next stop, the sweet village of Triacastela where the albergue has a ten-minute-a-euro leg massage chair in the common room. The rain sweeps in at night. In the morning, there are leaden-gray clouds that threaten, but fail to deliver, most of the day. I walk through ancient villages with houses made of native stone, the narrow streets home to sleeping dogs and feral cats, the fields dotted with cows and horses, chickens, pregnant goats. Two women with wooden staffs herd sheep on the road. I stand aside, along with a few others, to let them pass.

We pilgrims both disrupt the life of these villages and help sustain them with our euros spent on bread and cheese, oranges and cold sodas. I smile at one of the women. She doesn't smile back. I don't blame her.

The next day begins the final one hundred kilometers of the Francés. This is the most popular—and most traveled—section of this Camino route because it is possible to receive a compostela, the much-valued certificate of accomplishment given to pilgrims for completing the Way, by walking just this last sixty-two-mile section. When I thought about walking the Camino months ago, I didn't understand what the big deal was about this compostela. I would know what I achieved. I didn't need a document to prove it. But as I have walked and each day gathered sellos from albergues, cafés, and churches, filling the spaces on my folded credencial with these often beautifully designed and colorful stamps that chronicle my progress, I find I am looking forward to my own compostela. This I will get in Santiago after submitting my credencial to the pilgrims' office. This is a Camino ritual, and the Camino, with its deep Catholic roots, is all about ritual.

Those who choose to walk only this last section to qualify for the compostela, beginning in the town of Sarria and ending in Santiago de Compostela, do so for many reasons: They have only a week they can spare from their lives. Or hiking more than a week is not their idea of a good time. Or they may not be physically able to attempt more than this final section. Or perhaps they want to hike with children or grandparents. But as I walk this last section, I know there is another reason I see so many more people: the presence of the Camino tourist. The Camino message boards that I looked at only after I returned are full of discussions—often heated—on the subject of the tourist versus the pilgrim. On this final stretch of the journey, I encounter many tourists. I learn, by talking to a couple I meet outside a café in one of the villages, that they and three other couples hired a company, at considerable expense, to arrange this one-hundred kilometer adventure, from booking flights and transfers to securing private accommodations, from selecting restaurants to handling the transport of their luggage to providing a sag wagon to follow along, just in case. For them, it is a vacation, a mildly adventurous one, a social occasion, not the solitary, soul-searching experience others come for. I know I sound more-Camino-than-thou here—especially given my own less-than-true-pilgrim backpack transports—and I do think there is room for all. My only "problem"—as if I have the right to have a problem—is that I have become accustomed to seeing just a few people as I walk. And sometimes no people at all. I have become accustomed to the silence. Even when I walk with Kiki, we often walk in silence. When we pass others, we exchange the customary *buen camino* greeting and walk on. Now there is chatter and laughter on the trail as these larger groups walk together. But if Kiki and I walk fast, and especially if we leave the albergue an hour before dawn, we can almost always outpace the groups and manage to find stretches of solitude and silence.

The path itself this day is tranquil, pastoral, and at times so redolent of cow manure that I almost swoon. And not in a romantic way. Then the next day, there is a long, treacherous, rocky slot canyon, the sort of challenge that loomed large earlier in the trek and now seems not easy but familiar and doable. The challenge now is not physical. I have come through this month with the only injury a sore collarbone. I have been tired but not exhausted. I have been sore but not hobbled. I have more than occasionally slept badly, but I have slept, and I have slept enough to wake in the morning and do it all again. The challenge now in these last few days is mental. It seems I need to keep reminding myself why I am doing this. And it seems I need to get out of my own head and just walk. Then, serendipitously, the next wave of the storm rolls in and scours me of thought, and all I can do is try to stay upright in the wind-whipped rain that slants forty-five degrees. This is when a midmorning stop for a café con leche and a Spanish torta feels like a divine gift rather than just a four-euro purchase.

The storm moves through, leaving the air crisp and pristine and so heavily scented by groves of eucalyptus and forests of cedars that it is almost medicinal. The path changes again as Santiago grows closer. I am walking through more cultivated farmlands, with little villages appearing every three or four kilometers. The vastness of the landscape is gone. I miss it, and I don't. There is comfort and familiarity in this terrain that has been tamed by people.

It is the day before the Day, "the Day" being my arrival in Santiago de Compostela. I have been on the road—the dirt path mostly, the rocky trail sometimes, the paved road occasionally—since September 23. It is now October 25. I can barely remember not being on the Camino, not waking before dawn and walking, my back to the sunrise, into the dark western horizon. Tomorrow, it will come to an end. I am relieved. I want to sleep in a big bed in a room all by myself. I want to take a very long shower. I want to wear clothes I have not worn every day for more than a month. I want to eat an enormous salad. But I am also saddened. Tomorrow, this tough but sublimely uncomplicated life, this single-focused time-out-of-time, will end, and I will have to return to my real life, the husbandless, daughterless life awaiting me.

These long, long days I am now so accustomed to have been interrupted by quirks and surprises: that morning I stopped at an ordinary-looking coffeehouse to discover a back courtyard dotted with extravagantly feathered pheasants; that beastly walk into Burgos made endurable by the wizened Frenchman; that evening spent in the distressing but entertaining presence of the drunken mayor of Fly Town; the handsome Parisian who sang to me in a courtyard in Grañón. Some surprises are unwelcome, like that ridiculous hunt for the albergue that did and did not exist; this headline-making storm. And some are mixed, like this day, the day before the Day, when Kiki and I decide to walk extra miles so that we can be close to Santiago and time our arrival for the following morning. Morning has always been a magical time on the trail. I want my arrival to be magical.

Our destination is the village of Lavacolla, only six and a half miles from Santiago. Kiki, ever-flowing fount of knowledge, tells me that Lavacolla was where pilgrims of old stopped to cleanse themselves before entering the holiness of Santiago. Lavacolla, she says, could be translated as *washing the colon*. Or *rectum*. Later, I look this up. She's kind of correct, maybe. One theory is the name derives from *lava* (from *lavar*, to wash) and *cuello* (neck). *Colla*, in other words, has nothing to do with the colon. But still, there is the idea of cleansing oneself at the end of a holy pilgrimage. Another equally-as-convincing theory is that the village was named for its geography: *lava* (low pasture) and *colla* (hill). Regardless, the village is a hefty day's walk—eighteen miles or so—from our starting point, miles made less pleasant, despite the lush and fragrant landscape, by the unforgiving weather.

Yes, rain. Yes, sheeting. I have run out of whiny things to say. It's just a matter of soldiering on. Which is what we do.

We arrive at the village in the very late afternoon, soaked and starving, only to discover that the accommodation we had so carefully and thoughtfully advance-booked was not, in fact, located in the village of Lavacolla. This is not the same screwup as the O Cebreiro–Do Cebreiro fiasco. It is simply—and frustratingly—that the mailing address is the village, but the location is outside the village. What this means is another four or five kilometers of walking. In the rain. And uphill. I wish I were making this up. The last hour we walk in the dark, our path dimly illuminated by our headlamps. When we finally crest the last hill and near where the place is supposed to be, we see nothing. No lights. No streets. No settlement. Just the dirt path we've been traveling. We walk on. There is no plan B. A minute later, perhaps less, but in any event less time than it takes for the onset of a full-on freak-out, we notice a narrow side path. It is unsigned, unilluminated, and unpromising. But it's there. And miraculously, it is the path to the hostel.

We present our pitiful selves to the innkeeper, who is charming and multilingual and, best yet, standing at a reception counter that doubles as a bar. We eye the bottles, taking careful note. But first things first. The room, a double, is warm. We strip off our sodden clothes and drape them everywhere. The shower is hot. The hostel has a lovely restaurant—most fortunate, as there is absolutely nothing else around—which Kiki later quite correctly calls "needlessly amazing." We splurge, ordering a huge pan of paella to share. And we bravely order off the menu, asking if the kitchen could make us *pimientos de padrón* for a starter (a dish both of us love with a passion not normally associated with charred peppers). Yes, says our needlessly handsome waiter. We wash it all down with two glasses of very good vino tinto. It is by far the best meal of the entire journey. This, now, today, is the yin and yang of the Camino in a nutshell.

That final morning, we start off predawn, warm, dry, eager, not eager. With only a bit over ten kilometers, we should be in Santiago by café con leche time. Or not. Although the path seems particularly well signed now that we are so close to the end, we are, perhaps, a little less diligent, a little too sure of ourselves. We take a wrong turn and head two or three kilometers down a road before we realize our error. We grumble and backtrack. But because of this forty-or-so-minute unplanned delay, when we get to the fork in the road where we went left rather than right, we have an unplanned and cause-for-celebration meetup with Andre and Jo. People regularly appear, disappear, and reappear as the days go by, but these two have shown up more than many other casually encountered trail friends. I met Andre, a floppy-haired young British guy, a musician with a soul-sucking day job, on my third or fourth day. He was the only man (and the youngest among us) in an eight-bed albergue dorm, and we all teased him to make him feel more comfortable. A week later, apparently staying at side-by-side albergues, we found ourselves hanging our handwashed laundry on a line in the sun and reconnected. Then there was the surprise meetup, with Jo in tow, as the two of them had become travel buddies, in a bakery at a town that marked the halfway point of the journey. A week after that, again unplanned, we found each other walking down a backstreet of a town and went out for a drink together. Jo, whom I had immediately liked but had not really gotten to know, was a sunny-spirited, delightful UK health care professional who, I got the impression, had just ended a marriage. We all had our reasons for walking. If Kiki and I had not made a wrong turn, we would not now be walking into Santiago with these two lovely people.

There should be an orchestral crescendo as the four of us stride into Santiago. Instead, there is this: We are in the old part of the city, walking on a cobblestone street toward the main square when we hear the music. The street dips down into a short tunnel, and off to one side stands a man playing bagpipes. The tunnel is a powerful sound chamber. The music is loud but also mellow and resonant, somehow both haunting and triumphant, uplifting and melancholy, just like this moment. This piper, or one like him, is a Camino welcoming tradition, I later learn. And the bagpipes (*gaitas*) are an important part of Galician musical tradition. But in this moment, I know nothing of this. In this moment, it feels as if the pipes are there just for us, just for me.

We stop to listen to the piper, put a few euros in his hat, and walk through the tunnel, into the light, and out onto the Praza do Obradoiro. Across the vast public space, cobblestoned, patterned in rays of the sun, and one of the most beautiful plazas in all of Spain lies the cathedral—the end of the journey. It is a take-your-breath-away building, a wild mix of three architectural styles, more than three hundred feet long, and, measured to the tip of its two flamboyant spires, more than twenty-two stories high. I stand in the middle of the square, troublesome backpack off my tender shoulders, hiking poles clattering to the ground, next to Kiki, Andre, and Jo, but also separate. Alone. And I feel simultaneously significant—I did this big thing! Look at me!—and, in the (literal) face of all this history, all this religion, all this culture and tradition, absolutely, gloriously insignificant.

I take a selfie, sit down on the warm stones, and cry.

26

SHE LOOKS SO MUCH better than I'd thought she would, given what I know they did to her body. She is lying in a person-size cardboard box on a gurney in the small antechamber that opens to the room with the big oven. Her face is lovely in repose. She is, she was, such a pretty girl. Looking down at her, I can believe what my ER doctor friend told me—that she fell asleep, fell into unconsciousness without knowing what she had done, without knowing her future. There is no pain or tension on that face. I focus on the perfect arch of her eyebrows—she tended them so carefully—and her short, thick lashes. All but her face is hidden from view. A sheet covers her to her chin, shrouding the shoulder-to-sternum-to-pubic-bone incision they made and then stitched up. A soft white towel is wrapped around the back of her head, hiding the scalp incision they made to gain access to her skull. Someone from the funeral home brushed and arranged her hair, the part that can be seen. Her long bangs sweep across her forehead.

The boys and I, her brothers, stand there, looking at her, thinking our private thoughts. Every once in a while, someone's hand reaches out to someone else's hand. How do we feel? Sad. Angry. Weary of seeing yet another dead body. We have no words. I place a pocket-size woven bag, one Tom brought back from Peru, on her chest. It has a few stones in it. I think these are ones she gathered from her walks along the Nehalem River. I also have brought a small mesh sack filled with crushed lavender flowers from our garden, and a tiny stuffed animal cat. She loved cats. The cat she brought into our lives, Simon, is still with me. The cat she adopted at the beach, who went through a few name changes before he became Toby, now lives with GB in the van. I wanted him, but GB wanted him more. GB needed him more.

After a while, I step back from her body and look up at the boys. We nod at each other. I go out to tell Bethany that we are ready. The funeral director and I are on a first-name basis. I have become a good customer. She and her assistant have been waiting outside, giving us as much time as we want before what comes next. What comes next is the cremation. We can leave now and let the professionals do their job, or we can be part of what happens, staying with her until the last moment. We choose to stay. Bethany opens the door to the second room, and the boys and I wheel the gurney up to the mouth of the oven. It is not yet fired up. The gurney is set at the exact height of the oven opening, making it easy to slide the box with her body into the oven. If there is something to be said at a moment like this, none of us knows what it is. Bethany shuts the oven door.

Outside, it is a soft summer afternoon. Inside, the oven will now fire up to sixteen hundred degrees. In about three hours, what will remain of her are bone fragments, which, further processed, will have a fine, sand-like consistency. Her ashes. They must cool overnight.

I pick up the cremains—this is what the industry calls the ashes—the next afternoon. Bethany hands me the white ceramic jar I brought in the day before. It is a pretty piece of earthenware I bought originally for Lizzie to use as a compost container at the beach house. She never did. I thought it was slightly macabre but also darkly funny and fitting in a way the boys would appreciate but others might cringe at, that her ashes are now in a compost container. Bethany hands it to me. Lizzie in the jar weighs about five pounds. I put it, her, in the passenger seat and belt her in. And then, in an exercise of flagrant emotional masochism, I find the song Lizzie and I used to sing together in the car, the one Carole King and her daughter recorded together, and I sing it alone as I drive her home.

Lizzie is in her white ceramic jar. Tom is in his wooden urn that looks like a birdhouse. I place them together, touching, on the top of the piano. Before all this happened, I never would have thought what I think now: *Maybe up there, out there, Tom's energy and Lizzie's spirit can be together.* A few weeks later, after talks with the boys, and texts and calls with GB, I belt Lizzie into the passenger seat again and drive out to the beach. I didn't know what—if anything—to do publicly about her death. Orchestrating a "celebration of life," given what her life had become and how it ended, did not feel right to me. Announcing her death on her Facebook page felt wrong to me. I did not want even the remote possibility of FA being in contact. In fact, I didn't even want him to know what had happened to Lizzie. Yet doing nothing, or not *nothing* but doing only something very private, family only, also seemed wrong. GB cared about her. Maybe some other people from her roller-coaster life at the beach cared about her. I left it to GB to put out the word. He also chose the place, a small patch of beach, a hidden inlet, that vacationers didn't know about.

Jackson, Zane, and I get there first. I carry Lizzie in her white jar in one arm and a bottle of mid-shelf tequila in the other. We bring plastic cups, a bunch of rosemary from the garden, and a small cache of stones from Lizzie's collection. We set out a blanket in the warm sand and wait. GB arrives, pale-faced, disheveled. And for a while, maybe ten minutes, it is just us, the four of us, with nothing to say. Then a couple arrives who look familiar. It turns out they were Lizzie's coworkers at the dive bar, the place she initially loved, the place GB now works at trying to upgrade the kitchen. They have two kids, I remember. Lizzie made cakes for their birthdays. They tell me they had lost touch with her, that they wish they had known the trouble she was in, that they are so sorry. The woman is crying. Three other people come, one of whom, a waif of a girl, walks up to me and says she had known Lizzie for only a few weeks but oh what a good friend she was. The others hold back, say nothing. The last to arrive is a tiny, shriveled couple, almost toothless, who look to be in their late eighties. They hold on to each other as they walk very slowly across the sand.

I haven't planned much of a ceremony, but I have planned something. I pour plastic cups of tequila for everyone and invite people to say something if they wish. The crying woman says Lizzie—Liz, she says; no one but the family calls her Lizzie—had a big heart. One of the others says she was great to work with in the kitchen. The very old lady says my daughter was a "sweetie" and that she "treated her like a daughter." I learn later that the couple allowed GB to park his van in their driveway. GB, shy, man of very few words, says, "She meant everything to me."

The boys and I exchange looks. We are among strangers and don't want to share our thoughts. We will do that later, just us. Instead, I have chosen a poem to read, "The Thing Is," by Ellen Bass. It is about facing grief and loving life. I get through it without tears. It is important for me not to cry in front of these people. We drink our tequila. I ask them to choose one of Lizzie's stones and cast it out into the ocean. Jackson, Zane, and I wait for them to go, then walk out to the shoreline with the ceramic jar. We walk into the ocean up to our ankles. The ocean is always cold in Oregon. Today, it is fifty-two degrees. We each take small handfuls of Lizzie and spread her across the waves. Even when you don't believe in rituals, they are soothing. Later, I give GB a small ziplock bag of ashes that he can do with what he wants.

The rest of the summer, for hours on end, for days on end, for many weeks, I work to make a place for Lizzie on the property. I don't think she wants to be in a compost container on top of Tom's piano. I think she'd like to be at the foot of that big oak on the west side of our land, the tree that used to support the ramshackle treehouse Tom and I constructed, the one Lizzie, the queen, ruled over, ordering the boys below to do her bidding. The problem is, the narrow path to the tree is completely overgrown, and the patch of ground in front of the tree, maybe twenty feet square, is thick with blackberries and vine maple, devil's club and Scotch broom. Neither the push mower nor the riding mower can get through it. I try a grass whip and a string trimmer to no avail. And so I get down on my hands and knees with a pair of pruners and start working. I do not think of it as punishment—punishment for being the mother who could not save her child—but the work itself is punishing. I do not think, until much, much later, about the people who self-harm by cutting themselves, slicing their own skin to distract from emotional pain or to externalize emotional pain, to feel something when they are numb. But almost every day, making my way, inch by inch, through the thicket, I bleed. Every day, although I am careful, although I wear gloves, I score my forearms. I scratch, scrape, abrade. It happens so often that I don't stop to wash. I just bleed into the gloves.

The work is done by the beginning of September. There is now a small meadow, a clearing leading up to the tree. I start to create a skirt around its base, a combination of stones Lizzie gathered, stones from Tom and me, charms and pendants and bits of jewelry from a box she kept, an abandoned bird's nest, a madrone branch, smooth and sculptural. I have made a pretty place for her. The boys come. We stand around the tree remembering her: Jackson and Zane, with Henry, his son, Tom's grandson. When he is older, his parents will tell him Aunt Lizzie died because she took too much medicine. Which is heartbreakingly true.

Whatever I am doing, and for whatever reasons, conscious or subconscious, something is maybe beginning to happen. I am slowly allowing myself to understand just how many layers there are to work through, the sadness, the anger, the guilt, and how I will have to feel them, and how long this will take. But there is something else. It is an odd feeling, odder still to express it: I feel a small sense of relief. Under the tree, on our land, she is safe. She is not struggling with all those demons she thought she was trying to quell and instead creating new ones. I mourn her, I grieve for the life she didn't get to live, the things she didn't get to do, the places she never went. But for the first time in years, many years, I am not worried about her.

Three weeks later, I leave to walk the Camino.

27

IT WAS MID-NOVEMBER, COLD, wet, and COVID. The Delta variant had taken hold that fall, spiking the rate of infection, scaring us anew. Our family "pod" had so far remained disease-free through the height of the pandemic. Mostly, we huddled in our separate homes, spending almost no time in the company of others, spending hours on Zoom. Before we got together, we tested. A few months before, the news had been good. Vaccinations up; infections, down. But now, that fall, the mask mandate for public spaces was back in place. Limits on social gatherings were being enforced.

It had been a little more than a month since Tom died. His ashes were in that wooden urn sitting atop the piano he loved to play. That urn had prompted the only fight Tom and I had during the last months of his life. After the standard chemo didn't work, and after the Hail Mary three-thousand-dollar pills not only didn't work but made him sicker, after we knew there was nothing else to try, when it was clear this was the end, the boys and I met at a coffee shop to talk about what we wanted to do after he died. We weren't so much event planning—although we did do some of this—as preparing ourselves. Just talking, just saying some words out loud, helped us. As part of all this, I began to research an urn that would hold his ashes. The ceramic ones with the angels and butterflies and flowers and calligraphed *I'll hold you in my heart until I hold you in heaven* seemed gratuitously maudlin. There were glass-blown urns and urns decorated with jewels, American flag urns and Jesus-on-the-cross urns, and a line of urns that featured silhouettes of men in the act of some athletic endeavor (mostly golf). As grim a chore as this was, I laughed a lot. Then I came across a simple wooden urn, a ten-inch-high cylinder tapered inward in the middle, hand-lathed into a strong but graceful shape. It was made of a fine-grained, reddish-brown wood by a craftsman in southern Oregon. It could be repurposed as a birdhouse. It was perfect. I ordered it.

I was out running errands when it was delivered a few days later. The driver left the box on the side porch next to the door to Tom's office. This is where he stayed much of the day, reading, sleeping, sometimes, if he had the energy, sorting through papers. He came out and saw the box, which announced its contents, URN, in six-inch-high letters on all sides. When I returned, he was livid. "So, you see me dead already!" he said, yelling, accusing me of I don't know what. "You're thinking ahead, huh? Can't wait?" We were both so raw. It didn't take much to draw blood.

I understand now how just seeing the word *URN* would be a knife to the heart. Then, his words stung me with such force I was speechless. *How could you possibly think this of me?* I had chosen the urn with love and out of respect for how he had chosen to face his death. I stood there listening to him yell—he never yelled—then I turned quickly so he wouldn't see me cry.

Four weeks later, he was dead, and I was carrying the urn with me to the funeral home, where I handed it to Bethany before she led us out to the crematorium. It was the boys and I. Lizzie, who would be laid out on a gurney in a cardboard coffin just like Tom was that afternoon, in this room, was still alive. She would live another eight months. She didn't come for the cremation. Now I think it was because her addiction had taken over her life. Then I thought it was just too much for her to bear. Both, I guess, were correct assessments.

I don't think I want to see Tom in that cardboard box, but I look anyway. There is a stillness beyond stillness. No mistaking this for sleep or even a coma. It is a body, but it is an inanimate object. He is wearing that Pendleton flannel shirt and those jeans he had on when he died. In the pocket of the shirt are the sprigs of rosemary I placed when they came to get him. I want to touch him, but I'm afraid. Let's do it together, Zane says. So that's what we do. Zane lays a hand on the chest of the body that used to be his father. Jackson puts his hand on the knee. I place my hand on the icy forehead and then the cheek. I wrap my warm hand around his, which is cold and hard, like a stone in winter.

We have brought things with us to put in the box with him,

to be burned with him, just as we will do months later when it is Lizzie's body in a box. Ancient Egyptians entombed their dead with earthly possessions, believing they would be useful in the afterlife. So, too, did the ancient Chinese and the Vikings. I'd like to imagine Tom feasting in Valhalla. I envy those who believe in some version of heaven. I don't believe in the afterlife or in heaven. I believe in the first law of thermodynamics.

We bring these objects as an expression of love, of memory, and because we just want something of us to be with him in that box. And we want this sorrowful, painful moment to be infused with humor. That's the kind of family we are. Zane has brought a pencil and a piece of plastic string from a string trimmer, Tom's favorite landscaping gadget. Jackson brought a packet of nitrate fertilizer (the subject of one of Tom's books) and a small chunk of Douglas fir. We laugh at these choices. I have brought a little mesh sack with dried oregano and basil from last summer's garden. I would like it to smell good in that oven. I also have a photograph of our weedy front meadow, the terrain he traversed on the riding lawn mower, and a slip of paper on which I've written the lyrics of a Rockpile song that captured who we were at the beginning of us: "Teacher, teacher, teach me love / I can't learn it fast enough." I stuff these in his other pocket. And then we wheel him to the oven, and Bethany closes the door, and pushes the button.

The next day, I go back to pick up the wooden urn with Tom's ashes. "I don't know how to tell you this," Bethany says after ushering me into one of the private rooms. "But there was too much of Tom for that urn." She hands me a thick plastic bag secured with a metal tag. "Here's the rest of him." She knows she can talk to me like this. I love that she talks to me like this, like I am someone who sees the humor, appreciates and needs the humor, not someone whose arm she has to pat while saying soothing words that don't soothe. I grab the urn and the bag, and in the car on the way home, I talk to Tom and tell him I forgive him for yelling at me about the damned urn. I should have bought a bigger size, I tell him.

Picking up the urn does not make me cry. What makes me cry, ten minutes later, is coming across a half-empty bottle of Coke Zero in the back of the refrigerator and remembering Tom's cravings in those final two weeks. He was not a fan of any soda, but there was something about the effervescence of it, the iciness, that felt good, that temporarily soothed his cough. I look at the bottle sitting there. He poured from that bottle. That was less than a week ago. It feels like yesterday, and then it feels like years ago.

And now here is the urn again, sitting on a portable folding table on our back deck. The table is under an awning we've set up to protect people from the rain. Because: It is mid-November, cold, wet, and COVID, and, despite all this, we're "doing something" for Tom. He had never wanted to talk about a gathering, a wake, a whatever. "I'll be dead. Do what you want," is what he said. Not in a dismissive way. Actually, sort of funny. But also practical, straightforward, like he was about most things. His "final wishes" were not about hiring a bagpiper to play "Amazing Grace" but rather for us to use the energy he was releasing in death. So, it was left to the children and me to figure out what, if anything, we wanted to do. "The children" meant the two boys. Lizzie was only sporadically responding to texts and rarely to phone calls.

The boys reached out to her too and got no response. It was painful to not have her involved, but there was so much pain already, it almost didn't register. We, my sons and I, knew we needed to do something. It needed to be a marker of sorts, both for us and for the friends who cared about him. We decided on a very small gathering, outside, with a little ritual and a lot of tequila. It would be small not just because of COVID but because a big event was not our style, because we were a family of introverts.

I measure the back deck, calculate six feet between people, and figure we could accommodate fifteen under the awning and around the covered side porch. The guest list is as eclectic as the man himself was: the shaman couple with whom he traveled to Lesbos, Peru, and Iceland; the eccentric old physicist/inventor; the university archivist who tells bad jokes badly; the friend-of-decades and frequent lunch companion who knows almost as much about Carl Jung as he did; an old boss; a high school buddy whose issues have issues. And, of course, family: us, his sisters.

Zane is in charge of music (the Who, Dire Straits, Neil Young). Jackson is in charge of food (Thai spring rolls, broiled mushroom caps). I am in charge of tequila and ritual. The tequila is easy: reposado, of course, three bottles. The ritual is more challenging. I've been to a few celebrations of life, and they go on forever, and there's a lot of crying. No, and no. *What would Tom want?* I ask myself. Oh, that's right: nothing. I will make it up. Because stones are so important to me, and were to Tom, and were a big part of his travels with the shaman folks, I know I must do something around this. I put together a collection of fifteen of Tom's stones and lay them out on the table next to the urn. Also on that table is the big glass punch bowl we use once a year for our Christmas party. I fill it with water. I have an idea.

People arrive, some masked, some not. As they walk under the awning, I ask them to choose a stone from the table and hold it or put it in a pocket, to keep it close. At the end of the gathering, I will ask them to deposit their stone in the punch bowl. Water has so many meanings: cleansing, purity, depth, renewal—life. I tell them that the stones they hold, infused by their energy and their thoughts, will sit in the water for a while, maybe days, maybe weeks, and then be placed under the Fuji tree where some of Tom's ashes are buried. I will use the water to irrigate around the tree. That's all the ritual I can muster.

It starts to rain. We wait for one of Tom's sisters, but her plane has been delayed twice, and she won't make it in time. We wait for Lizzie. She promised to be here. Of course, I hoped—the boys hoped—she would show up. *She promised.* But she had promised many things. I text her in the morning, asking for her ETA, and get no response. I text her in the early afternoon just as we are setting things up and get no response. I think now how she must have struggled to leave the house, maybe dulling her pain with drugs, then falling into whatever state she fell into. She does finally get in her car and make the three-hour drive, arriving many hours after the gathering, when the family meets for dinner downtown.

Under the awning, people shiver in the damp, eat food, talk quietly to each other. Because Tom's friends represent the different parts of his life, his different interests and passions, some of these folks don't know one another. They trade Tom stories, all except the quirky physicist who loved Tom like a son and can't bear it, and he goes inside and starts playing the piano. He is good, very good, playing Chopin, I think. Outside, Mark Knopfler sings "Walk of Life." And even though Tom didn't want anything, or didn't care, I think he'd like this. The archivist who tells the bad jokes is crying, but everyone else keeps it together. Including me. I am sitting next to Karuna, the only person under the awning who never knew Tom. She is a casual friend who transformed, literally overnight, into my dearest, closest confidante, the one I call when I'm sitting in my car in the driveway weeping, the one who has driven an hour and a half four times this past month to see me, to sit and have coffee with me, to help anchor me in this world. It is a miracle of kindness.

The boys distribute heavy pours of the reposado, and I invite toasts. His friends are as smart and articulate as he was, and so are their toasts. Most are short. All offer a snapshot of what he meant to each person. My sons toast their father: Jackson keeping it short, holding himself tight, keeping his voice low, barely audible; Zane talking about how his father was always interested in and excited by what he did and how he wanted to be that kind of father to his own son. I listen but must turn away for a moment to breathe. They are old enough and life-experienced enough to know what an exceptional father they had. They have become exceptional themselves.

What had started as a drizzle had progressed to steady rainfall. We are huddling, as much as COVID-conscious people huddle, under the awning to stay dry. But then, as sometimes happens on late fall days like this in the Northwest, the skies suddenly lighten, the clouds part, and there's a temporary burst of sunlight. It feels like my cue. I'm up last. The cleanup batter, I guess. I have thought a lot about this moment. I knew that I did not want to give a eulogy. My deepest thoughts about this man I lived with for three decades are my own. Do I want to tell a touching anecdote from our past together? No. I want to preserve that memory for myself. The more public-facing and generic thoughts—how smart and kind and preternaturally curious and doggedly optimistic he was—everyone knows this. And so, I thank them all for coming. I thank them for being such important parts of Tom's life. And then I read a few lines of a Mary Oliver poem. "This is Tom," I tell them. Although Tom, as far as I know, never read (or heard of) Mary Oliver. "When death comes," she writes: "I want to step through the door full of curiosity, wondering: / what is it going to be like, that cottage of darkness?" The poem is not about death but about what comes later. Tom truly was curious, I tell them. You have to believe me. "He did leave wondering."

Tom always said we knew how to work a room, and he was right. And this is a "room," and I am now about to work it. I have one more thing to share on this suddenly sunny afternoon thirty-five days after my husband's death. I stop to take a sip—well, perhaps more than a sip—of my tequila and find my notes. Then I read this monologue by the comedian George Carlin:

> I want to live my life backwards.
> You start out dead and get that out of the way.
> Then you wake up in an old people's home
> feeling better every day.
> You get kicked out for being too healthy,
> go collect your pension,
> and then when you start work,
> you get a gold watch and a party on your first day.
> You work 40 years
> until you're young enough to enjoy your retirement.
> You party, drink alcohol, and are generally
> promiscuous,

then you are ready for high school.
You then go to primary school,
you become a kid,
you play.
You have no responsibilities,
you become a baby until you are born.
And then you spend your last 9 months
floating in luxurious spa-like conditions
with central heating and room service on tap,
larger quarters every day and then Voila!
You finish off as an orgasm.

Just as I finish, something happens: A small brown bat suddenly swoops in under the awning, flies straight through, and exits into the trees. I will now relate these facts. You be the judge:

Bats are nocturnal. They fly at night. They don't appear during the day.

Bats are masterful navigators (echolocation). They avoid humans and rarely come close to structures.

The bat was Tom's favorite animal (tied with giraffes).

The boys and I still talk about this moment, now years later. What was that? Was that what we think it was? Yes, I answer, it is what you, what we, thought it was.

28

I WOULD LIKE TO tell you that the Camino healed me. I would like to write a final scene, set on the plaza in front of the cathedral in Santiago de Compostela, that didn't end with me sitting on the cobblestones and crying. In this scene, in the soft morning light, my scuffed backpack by my feet, the toe boxes of my hiking shoes wrapped in duct tape, maybe a slight sheen of sweat dampening my forehead, the faintest of smiles would cross my face as I silently recited this Hemingway line: "The world breaks everyone, and afterward, some are strong at the broken places." If I wrote fiction, I would write this.

But real life is messy; the nuances are nuanced; the issues have issues. Real life is glorious and heartbreaking; so predictable that you find yourself asleep at the wheel; so full of drama and tumult that you cannot catch your breath. Maybe there's an arc to it, but you don't see it, because you are busy living it. Real life is full of lessons you ignore, and then learn you have to learn, and then learn, and then forget, and then learn again. Or maybe never.

I think of Tom every day. I miss him more now than I did last year or the year before. I miss him more because, now that he isn't here, I see him more clearly. That isn't a modestly clever turn of phrase. That is the truth. All he is, all he was in my life, has been distilled. What is left, this distillate, is purified high-concentrate Tom-ness. His essence. And I see what I too often did not see when he was alive, when I viewed him through the critical lens of daily life, the way two people, over time, can take all the big, important things for granted, which leaves plenty of time and energy to be pissed off about the things that really don't matter. Or that you realize, in retrospect, did not matter.

I think of Lizzie every day. When she was alive, especially during those last few years when she had become someone I could not reach, someone who did not want to be reached, I tried hard not to think about her. Now my life is a series of Lizzie moments. Some mornings, I hike in her BE STRONG, BE A GIRL T-shirt, the one I bought her in high school. I wear one of her silver rings on my middle finger. I have a playlist on my phone that she curated for me. I make the almond-and-coconut cake she introduced to our household. I live with and love the cat she brought into our lives. Sometimes, maybe too often, I wander into what used to be her bedroom to stare at the two shelves of ribbons and awards she accumulated through middle and high school: discus, shot put, wrestling, soccer. That scent I used to wear, Obsession? She loved it and could not afford it and bought a knockoff at Walgreens. I wear it still sometimes and always, always think of her.

And so, there is not a neat ending to this. The trail ends, yes. The Camino, with its forward movement through time, its slow but steady progress, its much-anticipated arrival at an iconic terminus, is satisfyingly linear. But the two lives that ended? There is not a finality to that. These two, my husband, my daughter, are so much a part of who I am, and who I will ever be. I am walking through the world with them and without them. There is no denouement. The story continues.

Lizzie's musical tastes were eclectic. She loved arena rock and death metal and techno. She listened to hip-hop and to country and western. She could sing along to Regina Spektor and Beyoncé. For a long time, one of her go-to songs was a semisappy, inspirational ballad, "Dream Big." I didn't understand what the appeal was, musically. I think the reason she listened to that song as often as she did was because she needed to hear the lyrics.

When you cry be sure to dry your eyes . . .
When you Dream,
Dream Big

She and Tom often talked about dreams. Her dreams had big plots and exotic locations and lots of action. She was often in trouble. She escaped, or she woke up. No one came to her rescue in these dreams. She recalled her dreams in astonishing detail. Tom listened and nodded but rarely commented.

He could have. He was a student of dreams. For more than a decade, he belonged to a men's dream group led by a Jungian therapist. The bookcase by his side of the bed held a collection of several dozen dream-analysis books. Tom often analyzed my dreams, which I thought were too straightforward and obvious to merit analysis, like the dream where I hit my father on the head with a frying pan. But he always found something worth thinking about. I miss that.

Tom rarely appeared in my dreams when he was alive, but that third night on the Camino, while I was sleeping in the bottom bunk in the albergue in Larrasoaña, he came to me, and I think this made up for all those years he never appeared. His message was clear and unambiguous. Even he, master analyzer, would have thought so. But more than that, his presence was palpable. I felt him. I felt the heat of his body.

A month or so after I returned from Spain, I awoke remembering this dream: Tom's friend, a shaman named Jón Ágúst, an intense, ethereal sort of man whom I had met when I tagged along with Tom on a trip to Iceland, was operating a huge piece of earthmoving machinery in the meadow in front of my house. It was an outsize bulldozer. He was using it to pile a mound of rich earth in the center of the meadow. I lay in bed, thinking: This is actually a dream that calls for analysis.

My view of dreams, nourished and enriched by years of talks with Tom, was that dreams were not random firings in the brain; they were a way for one part of you to communicate to another part of you: to send messages, alerts, prompts, pings. Subconscious to conscious. The stuff ignored, unexplored. Free from the external stimuli (not to mention ego) of daily waking life, the subconscious takes over when we sleep.

And so, I spent time with that dream, which to me was about unearthing what needed to be unearthed. It seemed to offer a clear message: Take this dirt, this earth, and make something new. I checked in with Carl (Jung, that is) about this. He agreed. The meadow might symbolize a place of growth, fertility, and the Self. The tractor, a powerful machine, might represent my inner strength and the active process of dealing with my emotions and the changes in my life. The act of moving earth could symbolize uncovering hidden aspects of the psyche and the transformative process of grief.

Oh, Lizzie, I get it: *When you dream, dream big.*

When I messaged Jón Ágúst about the dream, his shaman (not Jungian) view was this: The dream world is a conduit between the living-on-earth (me) and the no-longer-living-on-earth (Tom). He texted me: "I look forward to see if Tom sends clues about the meaning in the next few days."

The very next night, I had this dream: I was dancing ecstatically in the meadow (the same meadow in front of my house) with Henry, the baby Tom had held in his arms during the first year of Henry's life and the last year of Tom's. As I flung my arms around, I felt the wedding ring fly off my finger. I panicked. Since a month or so before his death, I had been wearing Tom's wedding ring on the middle finger of my right hand. It was too big for my ring finger. It was a little too big for my middle finger, but my knuckle kept it in place. In the dream, I looked down at my hand and saw the wedding ring was missing. I hunted for it, running back and forth across the meadow. I was distraught, in tears. I walked back to where Henry and I had been dancing, and I sat down on the grass. I turned my head, and there, right next to me, was his ring.

Tom and I had talked about whether we would be able to communicate after he died. The whole idea was so 1990 *Ghost*-y, so weird. But by then, everything was so weird already that the conversation seemed almost rational. I wanted these dreams—that first Camino dream, these meadow dreams—to mean that Tom had found a way to reach out to me and that I was receptive. I knew they were important, meaningful dreams, but were they *communication*?

A few weeks later, I awoke in the middle of the night from this dream: I am driving my car and realize I don't know how to get to my destination. The nav system isn't working. Google Maps is not showing up on my phone. Fine, I love paper maps. I stop the car, open the glove box, and look for a map. There is no map. For a moment, I think: *Shit, I'm screwed.* And then, just as suddenly, I am filled with some combination of curiosity and energy and joy. *I get to make this up*, I think. *I get to find my own way.*

Thanks, Tom.

Now go find Lizzie. She needs you.

Epilogue

GRIEF IS NOT A process. Fracking is a process. Baking a cake is a process. There are steps. You go through the steps. Each step leads to another. There is forward movement that results in a product, in a result.

This is not what grief is.

Grief is a thing, an entity. Grief is a new organ that has taken up residency in the body. Sometimes it causes discomfort like an upset stomach. Sometimes it is a dull ache like a bum knee. Sometimes the pain throbs and pulses, makes you sensitive to everything, feels unremitting, like a migraine. Sometimes this thing, this grief, is just there, a presence, a weight. You feel its weight. I will always feel its weight.

This new organ that is grief is many lobed, not just two like the liver; it is many chambered, not just four like the heart. It is not one thing. It is many: guilt, shame, regret, love, anger, sorrow, confusion, fear. Maybe that's why it weighs so much.

People tell me I am brave for doing what I do. But all this activity, all this doing, is my comfort zone, even if the details of the doing are challenging.

It is time now to do the very hardest thing, the thing I have been avoiding, the thing I am no good at, the bravest thing: to sit with it.

Acknowledgments

YOU GET TO KNOW a writer by reading her acknowledgments. At least I do. In fact, the first thing I do when I pick up a book is turn to the back to read the list: the appreciations and tributes, the kudos and shout-outs, the teachers, the parents, the paean to the partner who reads every word, edits like a pro, takes over domestic chores, qualifies for sainthood. Whew.

With that said, here is a window into my process, the journey of this book, and the people to whom I owe far more than the few words I offer here.

To Lydia Smith, friend, peregrina, filmmaker, to whom I owe my first awareness of the Camino and what it might offer.

On the Camino Francés, my gratitude to Emily Deahm for her care and kindness, to Joan Klaus for her verve and grace, to Susan Barg and her crew for laughs and good company, to Jo Walsche and Andre Kane for the intensity of time shared out of time, to Alexandre who rescued me from despair, to Federico who knew just what to do.

And to my hometown Camino de Ridgeline buddies, Ira, Martha, and Mia Aronin, for those random encounters that transformed into friendship, for that special trail energy that keeps alive the Camino spirit.

To Karuna Thompson, Claudia Johnson, and Julie Newton, who stepped in and stepped up when I needed them most—but had not learned how to ask. To Ann Black Goodman, who modeled resilience. To Bill Snell, for being there. To the older sisters of Kingy Boy (Cher Donnel, Morgaine Hager, Patricia Dant), for the painful, joyful sharing of love.

To those I do not know—but wish I did—whose work, whose words, challenged my thinking, made me smarter and stronger: Susan Cain, Bessel van der Kolk, Gabor Maté, Judith Grisel, Jonathan Gottschall. And especially, and for so many reasons, and always, Mary Oliver.

To my two ER doc friends, Jonas Pologe and Desmond Crooks. They schooled me in the ways of death and the body. But I owe them much more than the sharing of their medical expertise: To Jonas, who waited out in the office for hours, who placed his stethoscope on Tom's chest that night: We are all in your debt. To Des, with profound thanks for the abiding connection that comes from shared circumstance.

To Michelle Brewer, detective with a heart, mother who understood, calm in the storm. To Bethany Wozniak, a funeral director with a sense of humor, a woman I came to know too well. To Julian Gottshall, who cared when he didn't have to, who went so far beyond the call of duty that he transformed what began as a transaction into a friendship.

To Kim and GB, for the different and complicated ways they loved her.

To those who read or listened to parts of the book as it made its way, who offered both encouragement and advice: Kristina Padgett, Susan Tate, Ellen Todras, Kathleen Dillon, Geraldine Moreno, Eric Stachon. To my copyeditor, Sara Robb, who edited not just meticulously but with heart. To my cover designer, Terri Sirma, for beautifully translating emotion into art. What a team.

And now, my deepest debts:

To Kiki Lawson, KL to my LK, companion extraordinaire, amigo de mi alma, for what we owe each other. Oh, what we owe each other.

To Liza and Henry for bringing life and light to a dark place. To my sons, our sons, her brothers, Jackson and Zane Hager, for so many Negroni Fridays, for helping to knit together this family, for being the kind of men their father would be proud of, for just being.

To my ally, my friend, my comrade-in-arts-and-letters, sender of soup, believer in the power of story, believer in me, my champion, my literary agent, Heather Jackson.

To Renee Sedliar, the editor every writer dreams of: wise, funny, smart, meticulous, compassionate, intuitive, soulful, curious, sharp-eyed, tenderhearted. I could go on. There is so much *there* there. She gave a piece of her heart to this story. She has a piece of my heart.

This book began with a dedication to my husband and my daughter. I want to end it with an acknowledgment. This is not just an acknowledgment of their centrality to this story. It is an acknowledgment of the life we lived together, the best of times, the worst of times. And even then, so worth the living.

RAISING READERS

Books Build Bright Futures

Thank you for reading this book and for being a reader of books in general. We are so grateful to share being part of a community of readers with you, and we hope you will join us in passing our love of books on to the next generation of readers.

Did you know that reading for enjoyment is the single biggest predictor of a child's future happiness and success?

More than family circumstances, parents' educational background, or income, reading impacts a child's future academic performance, emotional well-being, communication skills, economic security, ambition, and happiness.

Studies show that kids reading for enjoyment in the US is in rapid decline:

- In 2012, 53% of 9-year-olds read almost every day. Just 10 years later, in 2022, the number had fallen to 39%.
- In 2012, 27% of 13-year-olds read for fun daily. By 2023, that number was just 14%.

Together, we can commit to **Raising Readers** and change this trend. How?

- Read to children in your life daily.
- Model reading as a fun activity.
- Reduce screen time.
- Start a family, school, or community book club.
- Visit bookstores and libraries regularly.
- Listen to audiobooks.
- Read the book before you see the movie.
- Encourage your child to read aloud to a pet or stuffed animal.
- Give books as gifts.
- Donate books to families and communities in need.

BOB1217

Books build bright futures, and **Raising Readers** is our shared responsibility.

For more information, visit **JoinRaisingReaders.com**

Sources: National Endowment for the Arts, National Assessment of Educational Progress, WorldBookDay.com, Nielsen BookData's 2023 "Understanding the Children's Book Consumer"